T0280110

BALTIMORE MONUMENTS

A HISTORY

THOMAS COTTER

THE
History
PRESS

Published by The History Press
Charleston, SC
www.historypress.com

Copyright © 2023 by Thomas Cotter
All rights reserved

First published 2023

Manufactured in the United States

ISBN 9781467153133

Library of Congress Control Number: 2022944976

CONTENTS

CONTENTS

FOREWORD

*I*n 1827, the president of the United States, John Quincy Adams, attended a fine dinner at Barnum's Hotel in Baltimore and ended his remarks with a toast to "Baltimore, the monumental city." It is the first time I have discovered the use of that phrase as the sobriquet for Baltimore, although it has been commonly used ever since in prose, poesy and even the brand of a cigar. The nickname referred precisely to two monuments, completed in about 1827: the Battle Monument at Calvert and Fayette Streets and the Washington Monument in Mount Vernon Place. Today, many people think that the name alludes to the many statues, monuments and memorials in our public squares and parks that followed, but in fact, our real claim to the use of that subtitle is that Baltimore was the first American city to build any public monuments at all. When President Adams made his toast, New York, Boston, Philadelphia, Washington, D.C., or any other sizeable city had nothing like them.

Perhaps that proud name inspired the proliferation that has given Baltimore more than its share of monumental public art, ranging from such a simple obelisk as the Wells-McComas Monument to the theatrical Francis Scott Key Monument on Eutaw Place.

Monuments, alone by definition, must be seen in the round and in the place for their true appreciation. We have a lot to be proud of in our monuments. Each one has a special meaning in Baltimore's history, and each one represents a deliberate aesthetic choice by someone in the past to improve the appearance of the city. Whether we find all of them truly artistic or agree with the taste of the past is no matter. The challenge is for us to go forth and do likewise, or perhaps better.

WILBUR H. HUNTER,
Director, The Peale Museum, 1946–78

ACKNOWLEDGEMENTS

*T*his book would not have been possible without the help and encouragement of many people. I must begin with Kate Jenkins, my acquisitions editor at The History Press, who provided great feedback and guidance. Special thanks to Rebecca Gunby, my good friend and former Baltimore City Archivist, for reading early drafts and providing feedback. Many thanks to the people who pointed me to valuable resources, including the archivists at the Baltimore City Archives, Maryland State Archives and the Smithsonian's Archives of American Art. I am appreciative of the staff of the Baltimore Heritage Organization for their valuable background information. Thanks to my daughter Stacy Aljabiry for her technical expertise. Additionally, thanks to my daughter Erin and her husband, Rob Stevens, for allowing me to stay in their home while I spent days strolling around Baltimore conducting my research and taking photographs. Finally, I wish to thank my wife, Sharon, who provided much-needed support throughout the project and assisted me with editing the final draft of the manuscript.

INTRODUCTION

*A*s a young child growing up in Baltimore, I routinely played in the city parks near my home. Located in those parks were several bronze and marble monuments that I passed frequently. In doing so, I often wondered why they were there, when they were put there, for whom were they dedicated or what event they commemorated. I knew that behind each monument there was a story and a piece of the city's historic puzzle. Many decades later, while working as an archivist at the Baltimore City Archives, I conducted research into these monuments that intrigued me long ago. After years of reviewing documented records in local, state and federal repositories, I was able to put together a concise history of Baltimore's public monuments. This book is the result of that effort.

Monuments and memorials adorn our public parks, squares and streets as permanent reminders of persons or events from the past. As the saying goes, "What is past is prologue." Through monuments, the deeds and actions of one generation are communicated to another. By their very presence, they produce a sense of pride in our citizenry and add beauty and distinction to our cities. They represent one way that people both remember and celebrate the past as well as shape the future generation's understanding of history. They primarily ask the viewer to remember. The word *monument* originally derives from the Latin root *monere*, which simply means "reminder." Cultural geographer Wilbur Zelinsky (1921–2013) broadly defined monuments as "objects that celebrate or perpetuate the memory of particular events, ideals, individuals, or groups of persons."

Baltimore has a rich and glorious history. From its beginning as a small town on the banks of the Patapsco River in 1729 to the present, the city has played a significant role in the development of the United States. To commemorate those persons or events that have contributed to Baltimore's and the nation's history, monuments have been erected throughout the city.

Ralph J. Sybert, a columnist for the *Baltimore News Post*, once wrote, "I fear many of us seldom devote even an errant thought to the great sacrifices of the people commemorated by the statuary of the monumental city. We often do not bother to learn who is memorialized on sculpture we see frequently."

The monuments and memorials of Baltimore have been studied by several scholars in the past. Examples include *Art in Baltimore, Monuments and Memorials* by William S. Rusk (Norman Remington Company, 1929), which covered Baltimore's monuments in an artistic framework. Another publication, *Public Monuments and Sculpture of Baltimore* by Henry and Carolyn Naylor (Maryland State Arts Council, 1985), produced a photographic inventory of Baltimore's monuments. In 1995, a study of the city's monuments from an ideological point of view was conducted by Melanie Davis Collier titled *Deciphering the Messages of Baltimore's Monuments* (College of William and Mary, 1995). As such, I was surprised to learn that there was no complete guide regarding Baltimore's monuments from a historical perspective.

Every day, thousands of city residents and visitors experience the rich, diverse culture of Baltimore. Over time, monuments have come to mean many things to different people. But increasingly, some of these monuments, particularly those honoring Confederate leaders and those connected with slavery, have become a painful and controversial reminder of the past. Historians have debated the issue for years, with some cities deciding to keep them intact and accept the historical figures for who they were, while others perceived them to be symbols of racism and oppression and removed them. Baltimore was no exception and debated what to do with the controversial monuments that many believed were not appropriate to be in the public domain.

During the civil unrest that followed the Charleston, South Carolina church shooting in 2015 and the killing of George Floyd in 2020, many monuments associated with racial injustice were destroyed or removed. Initially, activists targeted monuments associated with the Confederate States of America, its leaders and its military. The removal movement was driven by the belief that the monuments glorify white supremacy and memorialize a treasonous government whose principle was the perpetuation of slavery.

As the scope of the protests broadened to include other forms of systemic racism, monuments to Christopher Columbus were included in the removal effort, believing that he participated in the abuses against Native Americans. Confederate monuments and those honoring Christopher Columbus in Baltimore were either vandalized, destroyed or removed as part of the nationwide protest. Eventually, monuments honoring slaveholders Roger Taney and John O'Donnell were removed as well.

The responses to the removal of public monuments have been mixed. While many believe that the ideals they represented were unacceptable, others believe they represented their history and culture and should have been left to stand.

In undertaking this endeavor, it was not my intention to comment on the artistic merits of each monument or provide an opinion on any political controversies involving them, but to treat each one from a historical perspective.

EACH MONUMENT IS DISCUSSED according to the historical background of the person or event commemorated, its origin, designer, funding methods, controversies and a description of the monument itself. For the purposes of this book, I have limited the definition of a monument to an intentional outdoor structure that was erected to commemorate a specific person or event. I hope that the reader will enjoy *Baltimore Monuments: A History*, learn more about the people and events of this great city and perhaps discover interesting facts about Baltimore. I have enjoyed researching and sharing these accounts and hope that readers of this book will enjoy reading the accounts as well.

Chapter 1

ARTISTS AND ENTERTAINERS

EDWARD BERGE MEMORIAL

Location: Mount Vernon Place
Designer: Henry Berge
Erected: 1961

Baltimore sculptor Edward Berge (1876–1924) is honored by this enlarged replica of his *Sea Urchin* sculpture.

Edward Berge was born in Baltimore on January 3, 1876, the son of a marble worker. In 1896, he enrolled in the Rinehart School of Sculpture at the Maryland Institute College of Art. After graduation, Berge moved to Paris, France, and studied under Auguste Rodin for several years. He later returned to Baltimore, where he died on October 24, 1924. He completed more than seventy pieces of sculpture, many of which can be found in Baltimore.

In 1944, Frederick R. Huber, director of the Peabody Conservatory of Music, received approval from the board of park commissioners to replace Berge's original three-foot-high *Sea Urchin* sculpture in Mount Vernon Place with a larger one as a memorial to his friend.[1] Huber commissioned Henry Berge, Edward's son, to create the replica. In 1959, Huber donated $7,500 to install the larger figure, which measures seven feet, ten inches in height. The city accepted the gift, and in December 1960, the municipal art commission approved placing the larger figure in Mount Vernon Place.[2]

Edward Berge
Memorial, Mount
Vernon Place.
Photo by author.

The new bronze sculpture was placed in the Mount Vernon Place pool on December 4, 1961. The statue depicts a young female nude standing on a sea urchin shell with arms stretching outward.

The inscription on a bronze tablet reads:

> As a Memorial to His Friend Edward Berge, This
> Enlargement of His "Sea Urchin" by Henry Berge
> Was Presented to the City of Baltimore by
> Frederick R. Huber 1959 Completed 1961

BILLIE HOLIDAY MONUMENT

Location: Pennsylvania and Lafayette Avenues
Designer: James Earl Reid
Erected: 1985

Situated in a small park in the Upton neighborhood of Baltimore stands a bronze statue of the legendary jazz singer Billie Holiday (born Eleanora Fagan, 1915–1959). It was erected by the city government in 1985.

In 1971, a group of jazz artists and fans, wanting to honor Holiday in some manner, suggested building a drug rehabilitation center in her name. The plan never materialized, and after several years of inaction, the Upton

Planning Committee decided to erect a commemorative statue of her instead. The organization subsequently secured the services of local sculptor James Earl Reid to create it and selected the small park at Pennsylvania and Lafayette Avenues, near nightclubs where she once sang to packed audiences, as a location.

In 1978, the city government approved a preliminary grant for the statue using $50,000 of federal community development block grant funds.[3] Reid completed the statue in 1983 and prepared it for shipment to the foundry. At this point, however, Reid and the city government became locked in a dispute. Reid claimed that cost of the project exceeded the $50,000, while city officials argued that Reid had taken too long to complete it. Both sides threatened legal action but eventually reached an agreement.[4]

Original plans called for the eight-foot, six-inch bronze statue to be mounted on a bronze pedestal of the same height and covered with bas-relief designs depicting symbols of Holiday's songs. The pedestal, however, had to be scaled down to a simple, two-tiered, white base three feet in height. The statue was cast at the New Arts Foundry in Baltimore.[5]

More than two hundred persons attended the April 18, 1985 dedication of the Billie Holiday Monument. Lady Rebecca Anderson, a contemporary blues singer, accompanied by the Tracy McCleery Band, sang several songs popularized by Holiday. Mayor William Donald Schaefer delivered the main address, after which two relatives of Billie Holiday unveiled the statue.[6]

Billie Holiday Monument, Pennsylvania and Lafayette Avenues. *Photo by author.*

The inscription on the pedestal reads:

BILLIE HOLIDAY
1915–1959

Dedicated by
Mayor William Donald Schaefer
and
the Citizens of Baltimore
1985

CONRADIAN KREUTZER MONUMENT

Location: Patterson Park, Patterson Park and Eastern Avenues
Designer: R.P. Golde
Erected: 1916

This bronze, life-size bust of the famous German composer and conductor Conradian Kreutzer (1780–1849) was a gift to the city by the United Singers of Baltimore. The organization received the sculpture in 1914 by winning first place at the Twenty-Fourth National Saengerfest in New York City. Saengerfest is a singing contest between competing choirs. The United Singers of Baltimore can trace its origin to the old Liederkranz, meaning "garland of songs." The choir formed at the German Zion Lutheran Church on Gay Street in 1936, singing German folk songs in addition to church songs.

Sculptor R.P. Golde, a native of Germany and later resident of New York City, created the bust of Kreutzer in 1884. After winning the saengerfest, the sculpture was taken to Baltimore's city hall on August 10, 1915, by Louis Schneider and Fred Nordenholz, honorary president and vice-president of the United Singers. The bust was put on exhibition in the mayor's office until the municipal art commission could decide in which park it would be placed. One week later, the art commission and the board of park commissioners selected Patterson Park as the location.[7]

The $900 cost of the stone pedestal on which the bust rests was paid for by a benefit concert given by the United Singers of Baltimore on August 29, 1915, at Arion Park on Wilkens Avenue.[8] The pedestal, which was approved by the municipal art commission, is marked with rosettes and stands approximately ten feet high.[9]

Conradian Kreutzer Monument, Patterson Park, Patterson Park and Eastern Avenues.
Photo by author.

Dedication of the Conradian Kreutzer Monument occurred on June 15, 1916, with a presentation by Henry Thomas, president of the United Singers of Baltimore. Mayor James Preston accepted the sculpture on behalf of the city.[10]

The inscriptions on the pedestal read:

[FRONT]	[RIGHT SIDE]	[LEFT SIDE]
CONRADIAN	PRIZE SONG	PRESENTED
KREUTZER	AM	TO THE CITY
FIRST CITY	AMMERSEE	BY THE
PRIZE	BY F. LANGER	UNITED
WON BY THE	JOHN A.	SINGERS
UNITED	KLEIN	OF
SINGERS	CONDUCTOR	BALTIMORE
AT THE		
24TH		
NATIONAL		
SAENGERFEST		
BROOKLYN		
1915		

SIDNEY LANIER MONUMENT

Location: North Charles and 33rd Streets
Designer: Hans Schuler
Erected: 1942

Located at the entrance to the Johns Hopkins University campus stands a monument to the famous American poet and musician Sidney Lanier (1842–1881). It was presented to the city by the Municipal Art Society of Baltimore in 1942, the centenary of Lanier's birth. On April 30, 1940, the society passed a resolution to erect a monument in honor of Lanier and have it created by local sculptor Hans Schuler.[11] The following year, on October 28, 1941, the society selected North Charles and 33rd Streets as its location.[12]

More than two hundred people, including thirty members of the Lanier family, attended the dedication ceremony on February 3, 1942. R.E. Taylor, president of the Municipal Art Society of Baltimore, officially presented the monument to Dr. Isaiah Bowman, president of Johns Hopkins University. Mary Day Lanier, the three-year-old great-granddaughter of Sidney Lanier,

Sidney Lanier Monument, North Charles and 33rd Streets. *Photo by author.*

placed a basket of flowers at the base. In attendance were children from the Sidney Lanier School. Two of them, a boy and a girl, delivered speeches. Dr. Bowman pointed out that the monument faced east, place of the rising sun, which was appropriate for the artist who had penned the poem "Sunrise."[13]

The monument, cast in bronze at a cost of $10,000, depicts Lanier resting on a large boulder at the base of a tree. He is holding a pencil in his right hand while holding a writing pad in his left hand. His legs are crossed as if in contemplation. There is a field of flowers in the background with the sun shining above them. There are two female figures to Lanier's left, portraying music and poetry.

The inscription on the monument reads:

SIDNEY LANIER
POET—MUSICIAN
1842–1881

EDGAR ALLAN POE MEMORIAL

Location: Maryland and Mount Royal Avenues
Designer: Sir Moses Ezekiel
Erected: 1921

On the campus of the University of Baltimore stands a memorial dedicated to the famous American writer, poet and literary critic Edgar Allan Poe (1809–1849). Poe is best known for his tales of mystery and the macabre.

Plans to erect a memorial to Poe began in 1896, when Mayor Alcaeus Hooper called a public meeting to discuss the idea.[14] However, it was not until after eleven years of indecision and lukewarm response from the public that the final plans were eventually formalized. In 1907, a fundraising campaign was started by the Poe Memorial Association. Fundraising methods included circular appeals, lectures and musicals. Orren C. Painter, a teacher at Baltimore Polytechnic Institute, conducted a campaign of publicity to bring the movement to the attention of literary people, securing their aid. Painter also contributed $5,000 of his own money toward the campaign.[15] By May 1911, the Poe Memorial Association had enough money to secure the services of noted sculptor Sir Moses Ezekiel to create the memorial.

Soon after Ezekiel completed work on the statue in 1913, it was destroyed in a warehouse fire. He completed a second statue in April 1915, only to

Edgar Allan Poe Memorial, Maryland and Mount Royal Avenues. *Photo by author.*

have it broken into fragments by an earthquake at his Rome studio. In March 1916, a third statue of Poe was completed. However, the Poe Memorial Association did not want to risk shipment of it across the Atlantic Ocean while World War I was in progress. Sir Moses Ezekiel died in 1917, and it was not until April 1921 that the statue finally arrived in Baltimore.[16]

At the time of its arrival, a controversy developed between the Poe Memorial Association and the municipal art commission. The Poe Memorial Association wanted to place the memorial in the gardens located at Saint Paul and Pleasant Streets. The municipal art commission rejected that location and preferred the intersection of Saint Paul and Lexington Streets.[17] Both sides eventually agreed on the Maryland Avenue entrance to Wyman Park.[18]

Dedication of the Edgar Allan Poe Memorial occurred on October 20, 1921, attended by scholars and admirers of Poe from across the country. A short speech was delivered by Frances Turnbull, president of the Edgar Allan Poe Memorial Association. Turnbull formally presented the memorial to Mayor William Broening, who accepted it on behalf of the city. The memorial was unveiled by Eleanor Livingston Poe and Frances

Turnbull. Howard Kohlenstein, a baritone, sang a part of Poe's "Israel," accompanied by a quartet from the Peabody Conservatory of Music. Dr. C. Alphonzo Smith, professor of English at the Naval Academy and former Edgar Allan Poe professor at the University of Virginia, spoke on the life and writings of Poe.[19]

Nine years after the dedication, another controversy developed regarding the memorial. When Ezekiel carved the inscription onto the base, he inscribed the quotation "Dreaming Dreams No Mortals Ever Dared to Dream Before," taken from Poe's "The Raven." Many Poe admirers claimed that the quotation was inaccurate, noting that all accepted editions of the poem showed "mortal" in the singular. One such admirer, Edmond Fontaine, took matters into his own hands and chiseled the "s" from "Mortals" on the night of May 29, 1930. He was subsequently arrested and charged with defacing public property. The park board did not press charges, however, deciding that Fontaine had acted out of poetic justice.[20]

By 1982, time, vandals and the elements had taken their toll on the memorial. On February 19, 1982, University of Baltimore officials and members of the Poe Society appeared before the municipal art commission seeking approval to relocate the memorial to the University of Baltimore campus. The commission unanimously approved the request, conditional upon it remaining the property of the city on permanent loan to the university.[21]

The Edgar Allan Poe Memorial consists of a bronze statue of Poe approximately five feet in height. Poe is depicted as listening to the muses, who are singing him strange and far-off melodies. He is dressed in a gown and seated on a classic chair whose outer sides are marked by relief panels—to one side a muse hanging a laurel festoon and to the other a winged muse of music with thistles. The statue rests on a concrete pedestal six inches high and a concrete base two feet in height.

The inscription on the bronze tablet at the base of the memorial reads:

EDGAR ALLAN POE
19 JANUARY 1809 7 OCTOBER 1849
DREAMING DREAMS
NO MORTAL
EVER DARED
TO DREAM BEFORE

LIZETTE REESE MEMORIAL

Location: East 33rd Street and Stadium Place
Designer: Grace Turnbull
Erected: 1939

On the grounds of the former Eastern High School stands a memorial dedicated to Lizette Woodsworth Reese (1856–1935), a nationally known poet and author. A teacher in the Baltimore City Public Schools, she is most famous for her sonnet "Tears," which has been described as one of the most perfect sonnets in the English language.

Following the death of Lizette Reese in 1935, Grace Turnbull, a well-known sculptor and friend of Reese, decided to erect a memorial in honor of the poet. The grounds of Eastern High School, where Reese was once a student, was selected by Turnbull as a fitting location. For months, the students watched the artist at work. As the memorial neared completion, the planting of flowers, trees and shrubs which Reese loved and mentioned in her poetry, took place.

On June 1, 1939, Turnbull presented the completed sculpture to Eastern High School. The student body, faculty and guests assembled in the auditorium for the first part of the program. The memorial was formally presented to David E. Weglein, superintendent of public instruction. The entire audience then traveled out to the memorial site for the second part of the exercises. The program included the recitation of several of Reese's poems. Several sonnets and other poems written in appreciation of Reese were also read. Other parts of the program included the singing of three of Reese's lyrics set to music, readings by the Eastern High School Choral Speaking Group and the Glee Club's rendition of "The Lord Is My Shepherd." Dr. Elizabeth Nitchie, professor of English at Goucher College, delivered the main address.[22]

Throughout the years, the Lizette Reese Memorial has withstood neglect, vandalism and the elements of nature. In April 1987, with the Eastern High School closed, the memorial was moved to the grounds of Lake Clifton High School on Harford Road. In May 2009, the Eastern High School Alumni Association donated $20,000 to have it disassembled and moved back to its original location overlooking the grounds of the old Eastern High School (currently the Weinberg YMCA) on 33rd Street.

The stone sculpture depicts a hooded shepherd surrounded by a flock of sheep and his faithful dog by his side. In his arms, he is cradling a small

Lizette Reese Memorial, East 33rd Street and Stadium Place. *Photo by author.*

lamb. The base is made of pink Georgia marble. Turnbull received her inspiration for the sculpture by the recurring images of a shepherd and sheep in Reese's poetry.

The inscription on the base reads:

COME EVERY HAPPINESS
AND EVERY DREAD
YOU THAT ARE WOUNDED COME
OF POOR OR BUFFETED

HERE IS A PASTURE HERE
IS GRASS A COUNTRY WALL
YOU ARE THE SHEEP
IN NEED OF ALL

A SHEPHERD IS AT HAND
MOST COMFORTABLE OF LOOK
HE HAS A LONG-USED STAFF
HE HAS A CROOK

A SMILING CLOAK HE WEARS
SMILING OF THE GOD AIR
AND OF THE BRAMBLE BUSH
THAT REDDENS THERE

THAT ANCIENT TASK OF HIS
HAS MADE HIM WISE AND BOLD
HE HAS BEEN TENDING SHEEP
MORE YEARS THAN CAN BE TOLD
WISE BOLD AND TENDER TOO
HE IS OF SUCH KIND
HIS VERY SMILE IS TO THEM
WHO SEEK UNTIL THEY FIND

HERE IS A PASTURE HERE
IS ONE WITH WHOM TO STAY
HE'S BEEN TENDING SHEEP SO LONG
HE KNOWS A SHEPHERD'S WAY

IN MEMORIAM
1856 LIZETTEE WOODSWORTH REESE 1935

The inscription on the back wall reads:

> The Poet Lizette Woodsworth Reese was born and
> always lived in this vicinity. A graduate of Eastern
> High School. She taught for forty-seven years
> in the schools of Baltimore. This memorial was
> presented to the school by the sculptor
> Grace H. Turnbull
> June 1939

RICHARD WAGNER MONUMENT

Location: Druid Hill Park
Designer: R.P. Golde
Erected: 1901

On a grassy knoll in Druid Hill Park stands a bronze bust of the famous German composer Richard Wagner (1813–1883) surmounted on a granite pedestal. It was presented to the city in 1901 by the United Singers of Baltimore. The organization received it in 1900 after winning first place at the Nineteenth National Saengerfest, an annual choral competition held in Brooklyn, New York.

The bust was created by German-born sculptor and New York resident R.P. Golde. The municipal art commission, at its meeting on April 19, 1901, approved the design of the monument and gave the United Singers of Baltimore permission to place it in Druid Hill Park.[23]

Dedication of the Richard Wagner Monument occurred on October 6, 1901, attended by a crowd of more than thirty thousand people. Seated on a platform were members of the United Singers of Baltimore and invited guests. The United States and German national flags were situated on either side of the monument, with banners of German singing societies situated nearby.

Two instrumental selections of the "Hallelujah" chorus from "The Messiah" and Weber's "Jubal Overture" preceded the ceremony. Opening exercises included a thirty-minute concert directed by Professor David

Richard Wagner Monument, Druid Hill Park. *Photo by author.*

Malamet, who wrote the prize-winning song "Scheiden" that brought the monument to Baltimore. A prayer was delivered by Reverend Julius Hofman, pastor of Zion Church. The monument was presented to Mayor Thomas Hayes, who accepted it on behalf of the city.[24]

The inscription on the front of the pedestal reads:

> FIRST PRIZE
> AWARDED TO
> THE UNITED SINGERS
> OF BALTIMORE
> AT THE
> 19TH NAT'L SAENGERFEST
> BROOKLYN, N.Y. 1900
> PRESENTED TO THE
> CITY OF BALTIMORE

The inscription on the reverse side of the pedestal reads:

> PRIZE SONG
> SCHEIDEN (PARTING)
> BY
> D. MALAMET

Chapter 2

ATHLETES

ORIOLES LEGENDS MONUMENTS

Location: Oriole Park at Camden Yards
Designer: Antonio Tobias Mendez
Erected: 2012

In 2012, the Baltimore Orioles Baseball Team commenced the Orioles Legends Celebration Series by erecting larger-than-life, nine-foot-high bronze sculptures featuring six of the greatest Orioles of all time. Located in the Orioles Legends Plaza at Oriole Park at Camden Yards, the statues are the work of local sculptor Antonio Tobias Mendez.

FRANK ROBINSON MONUMENT
The first statue to be dedicated in the series was of Orioles all-star home run hitter and National Baseball Hall of Fame inductee Frank Robinson (1935–2019). It depicts Robinson at the end of a swing, the bat in his left hand trailing behind him. Thousands of fans packed the picnic area and nearby viewing areas of Oriole Park at Camden Yards on April 28, 2012, to see the unveiling of the statue. Upon seeing it, Robinson remarked, "This is a very special place in my heart, Baltimore."[25]

Frank Robinson Monument, Oriole Park at Camden Yards. *Photo by author.*

EARL WEAVER MONUMENT

The second statue to be dedicated was of Orioles manager and National Baseball Hall of Fame inductee Earl Weaver (1930–2012). Affectionately known by his fans as the "Earl of Baltimore," the statue depicts a customary stance of Weaver with his hands stuffed in his back pockets. Thousands of fans attended the unveiling of the statue on June 30, 2012. Upon seeing the statue unveiled, Weaver remarked, "It is great to be remembered."[26]

JIM PALMER MONUMENT

The third statue to be dedicated was of Orioles all-star pitcher and National Baseball Hall of Fame inductee Jim Palmer (1945–). It depicts the right-handed pitcher in full windup with his trademark high-leg kick about to throw a pitch. Palmer was present for the unveiling of his statue before a large crowd attending the Orioles baseball game on July 14, 2012. Upon seeing the statue, Palmer remarked, "To me, the theme of these statues is not about what I did…we just had really special people."[27]

Earl Weaver Monument, Oriole Park at Camden Yards. *Photo by author.*

Jim Palmer Monument, Oriole Park at Camden Yards. *Photo by author.*

EDDIE MURRAY MONUMENT

The fourth statue to be dedicated was of Orioles all-star first baseman, home run slugger and National Baseball Hall of Fame inductee Eddie Murray (1956–). It depicts Murray crouching with a bat in his hands, ready to swing. The statue was unveiled before a large crowd attending the Orioles baseball game on August 11, 2012. The crowd ignited into a thunderous applause as Murray waved and witnessed the unveiling of his statue.[28]

CAL RIPKEN JR. MONUMENT

The fifth statue to be dedicated was of Orioles all-star infielder and National Baseball Hall of Fame inductee Cal Ripken Jr. (1960–). Known as the "Iron Man" because he played in 2,632 consecutive games, the statue depicts Ripken about to catch a ground ball. It was unveiled before a large crowd attending the Orioles baseball game on September 6, 2012. Upon seeing the unveiling of the statue, Ripken remarked, "I'm very proud of that pose, it looks like me and I think it captures who I was as a shortstop."[29]

BROOKS ROBINSON MONUMENT

The sixth and final statue to be dedicated in the series was of Orioles all-star third baseman and National Baseball Hall of Fame inductee Brooks Robinson (1937–). The statue depicts Robinson ready to field a ground ball. It was unveiled by his fellow Orioles legends Frank Robinson, Earl Weaver, Jim Palmer, Eddie Murray and Cal Ripken Jr. before a large crowd attending the Orioles baseball game on September 29, 2012. Following the ceremony, Robinson was presented with a small replica of the statue.[30]

BROOKS ROBINSON MONUMENT

Location: Russell Street and Washington Boulevard
Designer: Joseph Sheppard
Erected: 2011

On October 22, 2011, with a large crowd in attendance, the Baltimore Orioles dedicated a bronze, life-size statue of their all-star third basemen Brooks Robinson (1937–) in the plaza across from Oriole Park at Camden Yards. It was created in Italy by Baltimore sculptor Joseph Sheppard and

Top: Eddie Murray Monument, Oriole Park at Camden Yards. *Photo by author.*

Middle: Cal Ripken Jr. Monument, Oriole Park at Camden Yards. *Photo by author.*

Bottom: Brooks Robinson Monument, Oriole Park at Camden Yards. *Photo by author.*

Brooks Robinson Monument, Russell Street and Washington Boulevard. *Photo by author.*

erected under the auspices of the Dorothy L. and Henry A. Rosenberg Jr. Foundation and the Babe Ruth Birthplace Foundation.

The ceremony began with a welcoming address by local sportscaster Scott Garceau, followed by a recitation of the Pledge of Allegiance from Boy Scout Troop 315. The national anthem was sung by Lauren Hayes, granddaughter of Robinson's friend and teammate, shortstop Ron Hansen. Addresses were delivered by Maryland governor Martin O'Malley, Senator Barbara Mikulski, Henry Rosenberg Jr., Mayor Stephanie Rawlings-Blake and Jeff Idelson, president of the National Baseball Hall of Fame. The sculptor, Joseph Sheppard, along with members of the Robinson family, unveiled the statue. The final address was made by Robinson himself, thanking everyone for the honor.[31]

The 1,500-pound bronze statue depicts Robinson with a baseball in his hand, ready to throw out a runner. The pose was gleaned by Sheppard's examination of historical photographs, as well as interviews between Sheppard and Robinson.

The inscription on the south side of the pedestal reads:

B. ROBINSON 5

Brooks Calbert Robinson

Baltimore Orioles 3rd Baseman
1955–1977

The inscription on the west side of the pedestal reads:

Brooks Robinson was born in Little Rock, Arkansas, but he became Baltimore's hometown hero. Arriving here in September 1955 at the age of 18, he went on to spend all or part of 23 seasons with the Baltimore Orioles, along the way becoming the heart and soul of the franchise.

The all-time third baseman played in 18 All-Star games, won 16 Gold Glove Awards and the 1970 World Series MVP. He was named Most Valuable Player in 1960, '62, '64, and was co-winner with Frank Robinson in 1971.

Baseball's "Human Vacuum Cleaner" set 10 major league fielding records, and three American League records for third basemen, including highest lifetime fielding percentage (.971). He was voted into the National Baseball Hall of Fame in 1983.

The inscription on the east side of the pedestal reads:

Brooks Robinson was the second person to ever receive the Roberto Clemente Award, granted to the baseball player who best exemplifies the game of baseball, sportsmanship, community involvement, and the individual's contribution to his team.

In 1970, Brooks was named the S. Rae Hickok Professional Athlete of the year, an award granted to the top professional athlete in all United States sports that year. Brooks was elected in 1999 to the Major League Baseball All-Century Team—the best players at each position from 1900 through 1999.

"There's not a man who knows him who wouldn't swear for his integrity and honesty and give testimony to his consideration of others. He's an extraordinary human being, which is important, and the world's greatest third baseman of all time, which is incidental."
Sportswriter John Steadman

RAY LEWIS MONUMENT

Location: M&T Bank Stadium Plaza
Designer: Frederick Kail
Erected: 2014

The Baltimore Ravens honored their most famous player, Pro Football Hall of Fame inductee Ray Lewis (1975–), by erecting this bronze likeness of him in the plaza of M&T Bank Stadium. Lewis played all seventeen years of his professional football career as a linebacker for the Baltimore Ravens and is considered to be the greatest player in the team's history.

The Ray Lewis statue, created by local sculptor Frederick Kail, was officially dedicated before a large crowd on September 4, 2014. In his remarks, Lewis said, "I'm never leaving Baltimore. I will forever be part of this city." Team owner Steve Bisciotti also spoke at the event, saying, "We are witnesses to the greatest leader in the history of the NFL."[32]

Ray Lewis Monument, M&T Bank Stadium Plaza. *Photo by author.*

The nine-foot-high, 1,200-pound statue depicts Lewis in his football uniform, frozen in mid-step and doing his famous entrance to the field that so many Ravens fans were accustomed to seeing. The statue surmounts a black marble pedestal with an inscription that simply reads:

Ray Lewis

GEORGE "BABE" RUTH MONUMENT

Location: Oriole Park at Camden Yards
Designer: Susan Luery
Erected: 1995

This bronze, larger-than-life-size statue, referred to as "Babe's Dream," was erected in 1995 by the Maryland Stadium Authority in honor of baseball legend and National Baseball Hall of Fame inductee, George Herman "Babe" Ruth (1895–1948). Although he became famous as a New York Yankee, his roots are in Baltimore, where he grew up and learned how to play baseball.

The sculptor, Baltimore-born Susan Luery, attended the Maryland Institute College of Art. She researched Ruth by reading books and speaking to people with knowledge about Babe Ruth and baseball. Luery also had a lookalike model come to her studio while she worked on the

George "Babe" Ruth Monument, Oriole Park at Camden Yards. *Photo by author.*

statue. It took her seven months to form a twenty-eight-inch model before creating the large-scale version. She produced the nine-foot statue a year later, in 1994. It was placed in Camden Yards on February 6, 1995, Ruth's 100th birthday.

The Babe Ruth statue was officially unveiled during an Orioles game on May 15, 1995. Ruth's daughter, Julia Ruth Stevens, and Luery threw out the game ball in celebration.[33]

Ruth is depicted how he looked in 1914, when he signed with his hometown team, the International League Baltimore Orioles. He is leaning on a bat and clutching a right-handed fielder's glove on his hip. Just prior to the statue's completion, however, it was discovered that it contained an error. Ruth was clutching a right-handed fielder's glove, but Ruth threw left-handed. By the time the error was caught, it was too late, as the statue was in the foundry and waiting to be completed. The statue remains with the error today.

The bronze tablet on the front of the pedestal reads:

BABE'S DREAM
George Herman "Babe" Ruth
Baltimorean
February 6, 1895–August 16, 1948

JOHNNY UNITAS MONUMENT

Location: M&T Bank Stadium Plaza
Designer: Frederick Kail
Erected: 2002

Located at the main entrance to M&T Bank Stadium stands a bronze statue dedicated to the legendary Baltimore Colts quarterback Johnny Unitas (1933–2002). The Pro Football Hall of Fame inductee was known as the "Golden Arm" by his many fans.

In 1999, Frederick Kail, a Baltimore sculptor and friend of Unitas, sought approval from the Maryland Stadium Authority to create a statue of the famous quarterback and place it in front of Baltimore Raven's Stadium. The authority gave its approval in 2000 and established the Tribute to Johnny Unitas Committee to raise the necessary funds. Headed by Baltimore businessman Ted Bauer and former Baltimore Colts players Bruce Laird

Johnny Unitas Monument, M&T Bank Stadium Plaza. *Photo by author.*

and Elmer Wingate, the committee met its goal within eighteen months through the generosity of the local business and community organizations.

The Johnny Unitas statue was officially dedicated on October 20, 2002, thirty-nine days after his death. Many of Unitas's former teammates attended the ceremony. At the unveiling, his widow, Sandra Unitas, said, "The Unitas family is pleased and touched by the establishment of Unitas Plaza."[34] The fourteen-foot statue weighs two thousand pounds and depicts Unitas cocking his arm, poised to throw.

The inscription on the pedestal reads:

JOHNNY UNITAS
THE GOLDEN ARM

Chapter 3

CIVIC LEADERS

Chapin Harris Monument

Location: Wyman Park and Art Museum Drives
Designer: Edward Berge
Erected: 1922

Chapin Harris (1806–1860), the "Father of American Dentistry," is honored by this portrait bust. In 1840, Harris founded the Baltimore College of Dental Surgery, the first dental college in the United States.

The idea for a monument honoring Chapin Harris originated in 1911 with Dr. William G. Foster, dean of the Baltimore College of Dental Surgery. Foster persuaded the Maryland State Dental Association to establish a seven-member Harris Monument Fundraising Committee, of which he was the chairperson.[35] The committee solicited donations from colleges, dental associations and individuals from around the world.

The project received a minor setback in 1917 when the United States entered World War I. The fundraising effort resumed following the war. In 1922, the committee secured the services of world-renowned artist Edward Berge to create the monument and selected the intersection of Cathedral and Preston Streets as a location.[36] That same year, following a joint meeting of the municipal art commission and the board of park commissioners, the proposed location was changed to the intersection of Linden and North Avenues.[37]

A minor controversy developed when the park board and its president, J. Cookman Boyd, approved Berge's design with the stipulation that a

Chapin Harris
Monument,
Wyman Park
and Art Museum
Drives. *Photo by
author.*

proposed wreath on the front of the pedestal be removed or altered. The stipulation stirred a resentment among local artists, who perceived it to be usurpation of authority.[38] Noted Baltimore sculptor Hans Schuler stated, "I think Mr. Boyd went too far. As I understand it, his duty is to select a site, attend to the shrubbery, surroundings, and grading and see that a proper situation is created. I do not believe that it is his duty to pass on the actual quality of the monument."[39]

Berge relented and replaced the wreath with a pair of torches. The Chapin Harris Monument was officially dedicated on June 1, 1922, by members of the National Alumni Association of the Baltimore College of Dental Surgery. Dr. William G. Foster presided over the exercises, which included addresses by Dr. Timothy Heatwole and Dr. Harvey Burkhart, former president of the National Dental Association. Dr. Burkhart presented the monument to Mayor William Broening, who accepted it on behalf of the city. The exercises concluded with an invocation by Reverend Henry Sharp.[40]

In 1937, the Maryland State Dental Association, dissatisfied with the North and Linden Avenues location, believing that it was too obscure for such a distinguished person, proposed a new location. In 1939, the board of park commissioners approved moving it to the intersection of Wyman Park and Art Museum Drives across from the campus of Johns Hopkins University.[41]

The monument stands ten feet, eight inches in height. The bronze bust is three feet, six inches in height and surmounts a granite pedestal seven feet, two inches in height. A pair of bronze torches are attached to the front of the pedestal.

The inscription on the front of the pedestal reads:

HARRIS
1806–1860

The inscription on a bronze tablet located on the back of the pedestal reads:

Chapin A. Harris
scholar teacher man
of vision and untiring
energy. A pioneer
organizer of professional
dentistry. The
first dental college
in the world founded
in Baltimore 1839

Committee
Dr. W.G. Foster, chairman
Dr. T.O. Heatwole, Dr. H.A. Wilson
Dr. J.W. Smith, Dr. W.W. Dunbracco
Dr. M.G. Sykes, Dr. Geo. E. Hardy

JOHN MIFFLIN HOOD MEMORIAL

Location: Preston Gardens, Saint Paul and Saratoga Streets
Designer: Richard E. Brooks
Erected: 1911

In 1911, in recognition of more than a quarter century of service to Baltimore, the city government erected a bronze statue of John Mifflin Hood (1843–1906). The memorial stands in Preston Gardens, an area that Hood helped rebuild after the Great Baltimore Fire of 1904.

John Mifflin Hood was a prominent Baltimore businessman and president of the Western Maryland Railroad. After the fire of 1904 destroyed the entire business district of Baltimore, Hood recommended that the city government sell its Western Maryland Railroad stock and use the money

John Mifflin Hood Memorial, Preston Gardens, Saint Paul and Saratoga Streets. *Photo by author.*

to rebuild the burned area. He worked tirelessly and convinced many of his wealthy friends to contribute to the effort. Hood spent the last two years of his life devoted to the cause.

In 1907, to show its appreciation, the city government appropriated $10,000 toward the erection of a memorial in honor of Hood. The money was part of the unused proceeds derived from the sale of the Western Maryland Railroad stock.[42] News of the proposed memorial caused considerable discussion in the city's art community, many of whom wanted a local artist to do the work. The widow of John Mifflin Hood preferred Edward Virginius Valentine, a well-known sculptor from Virginia, and offered a $10,000 contribution toward the pedestal if he were selected.[43]

The four-member John Mifflin Hood Memorial Commission, appointed by the mayor and city council to oversee the project, awarded the contract to Richard E. Brooks of New York.[44] Commission member William B. Hurst, after being impressed by a recent work of Brooks, convinced other commission members to select him.

As a location, the commission selected the intersection of Sharp and Baltimore Streets, which received the endorsement of the municipal art commission as well as the mayor and city council.[45] This seemed an appropriate location, being in the area that Hood helped rebuild after the great fire.

Dedication of the John Mifflin Hood Memorial occurred on May 11, 1911, with a concert given by Steinwald's Band preceding the ceremony. Hood family members and invited guests occupied a stand on the west side of the memorial. These included city and state officials, railroad men, members of civic and patriotic societies, officials of the United Railways (of which Hood was a former president) and personal friends of Hood.

The exercises were brief, with General Andrew Trippe, chairman of the Hood Memorial Commission and lifelong friend of Hood, delivering the main address. John Mifflin Hood III, the grandson of John Mifflin Hood, unveiled the statue. Mayor J. Barry Mahool accepted the memorial on behalf of the citizens of Baltimore.[46]

The bronze statue is nine feet high and surmounts a twelve-foot-high pedestal of unpolished Tennessee marble. Hood is depicted standing, holding a document in his left hand. Behind him is located the broken wheel of a railroad car with oak leaves, symbolizing the condition of the Western Maryland Railroad when Hood became its president. A bronze wreath of oak leaves adorns the front of the pedestal. A frieze encircles the pedestal that includes a large driving wheel, the headlight of an engine and the wheel of a passenger car. A surveying instrument is etched into the back of the pedestal.

To make way for an urban renewal project in 1963, the city government moved the memorial to Preston Gardens, Saint Paul and Saratoga Streets.

The inscription on the pedestal reads:

JOHN MIFFLIN HOOD

PRESIDENT
WESTERN MARYLAND
RAILROAD
1874 TO 1902

ERECTED BY
THE
CITY OF BALTIMORE
1911

JOHNS HOPKINS MEMORIAL

Location: North Charles and 33ʳᵈ Streets
Designer: Hans Schuler, William G. Beecher
Erected: 1935

Located near the university that bears his name stands a memorial in honor of Baltimore philanthropist and benefactor Johns Hopkins (1795–1873). It was presented to the city in 1935 by the Municipal Art Society of Baltimore, a private organization committed to providing "adequate sculpture and pictorial decorations and ornaments for the public buildings, streets, and open spaces in the city of Baltimore."

On October 11, 1904, the board of directors of the society voted unanimously to "secure subscriptions to an amount not less than $15,000 for the purpose of erecting a suitable memorial to the late Johns Hopkins" and appointed a seven-member committee to oversee the project.[47]

In 1913, after having obtained the necessary funds, the Hopkins Memorial Committee commissioned well-known Baltimore sculptor Hans Schuler to design and create the memorial.[48] It was the desire of committee member Theodore Marburg that the design feature running water, to symbolize the life and character of Johns Hopkins and to make it a living testimonial to his works. To accomplish this goal, Schuler engaged the services of noted architect William Gordon Beecher.

When the United States entered World War I in 1917, plans for the memorial came to a halt. At the conclusion of the war, work on the project languished for another ten years until December 1928, when Schuler presented his design to the committee.

The original intention of the society was to place the memorial on that part of the Johns Hopkins University campus known as "the bowl." The trustees of the university, however, opposed any portrait statue being erected on the grounds of the university. As an alternate site, the society selected a circular grass plot donated by the city government at the intersection of North Charles and 34ᵗʰ Streets.[49]

The Municipal Art Society of Baltimore approved a modified version of Schuler's design in May 1934, after having rejected the original design six months earlier. The revised plan consisted of one central pillar instead of four.[50] The running water feature required unusual care and exhaustive planning. The work had to be done exactly right without the possibility of future difficulties in its operation. The task of installing the pumping

Johns Hopkins Memorial, North Charles and 33rd Streets. *Photo by author.*

equipment, piping and drainage required was given to Frank Knell, one of the most trusted plumbing contractors in the city. The firm of Ruhlman and Wilson furnished and constructed the stonework according to the designs of Schuler and Beecher. The bronze work was accomplished by the Roman Bronze Works of Corona, New York.

Several hundred people attended the hourlong dedication ceremony of the Johns Hopkins Memorial on September 18, 1935. The exercises opened with an address by Douglas H. Gordon, assistant U.S. attorney and president of the Municipal Art Society of Baltimore. Mayor Howard Jackson, in accepting the memorial on behalf of the city, spoke of the accomplishments of Johns Hopkins and his legacy to Baltimore. Dr. Isaiah Bowman, president of Johns Hopkins University, delivered the main address.[51]

The Johns Hopkins Memorial consists of a single concrete column, twenty-four feet in height, with a fountain of running water at its base. It is surmounted by a bronze bust of Hopkins, six feet in height. On each side of the column rests a bronze allegorical figure in a seated position. The male figure on the left is in the pose of a thinker, symbolizing learning and the university founded by Hopkins. The female figure on the right side holds a medicine cup and a serpent, symbolizing the hospital founded by Hopkins.

The memorial remained at its original location until 1954, when, to eliminate a traffic hazard, it was moved to its present location on the Homewood campus of Johns Hopkins University on 33rd Street.

The inscription on the shaft reads:

JOHNS HOPKINS
1795–1873

SEVERN TEACKLE WALLIS MONUMENT

Location: Mount Vernon Place
Designer: Laurent Marquestre
Erected: 1906

Located in Baltimore's historic Mount Vernon Place stands a bronze statue of the famous Maryland lawyer, orator, reformer, linguist and poet Severn Teackle Wallis (1816–1894). Historians have referred to Wallis as the "Pride and ornament of the Baltimore Bar."

Severn Teackle Wallis Monument, Mount Vernon Place. *Photo by author.*

On May 24, 1900, the directors of the Municipal Art Society of Baltimore unanimously passed the following resolution:

> *Whereas the distinguished services rendered this community by the late Severn Teackle Wallis, and the close association of his name with the art and literature of this state, prompt us to erect to his memory a statue as a permanent memorial of his life; be it therefore resolved, that the Municipal Art Society of Baltimore subscribe the sum of $1,000 towards the erection of an outdoor statue to the late Severn Teackle Wallis and that a committee of seven be appointed...to solicit subscriptions for same.[52]*

The committee commissioned French sculptor Laurent Marquestre, a professor at the Beaux-Arts school in Paris. Marquestre was selected on the advice of George A. Lucas, a close friend of Wallis who spent many years in Paris.[53] Marquestre, who had never seen the subject, was able to create a statue in the perfect likeness of Wallis. The success was due to the way committee member Solomon Warfield collected and sent him information, photographs and even the clothes of Wallis.[54] At its meeting held on July 5, 1905, the board of park commissioners approved Mount Vernon Place as the location.[55]

On January 9, 1906, in the presence of approximately three hundred people, the Severn Teackle Wallis Monument was dedicated in Mount Vernon Place. The ceremony opened as Solomon Warfield introduced Arthur G. Brown, son of former Baltimore mayor George W. Brown and close friend of Wallis. Brown delivered an address highlighting the life and career of Wallis and called him an "ideal Baltimorean." The monument was presented to Mayor E. Clay Timanus, who accepted it on behalf of the city. The exercises concluded when Severn Teackle Wallis II, grandson of Wallis, unveiled the statue.[56]

The inscription on the pedestal reads:

SEVERN TEACKLE WALLIS
1816–1894

Chapter 4

CONTROVERSIAL MONUMENTS
THAT HAVE BEEN REMOVED

Throughout the years, monuments dedicated to Confederate leaders and other historical figures who owned slaves or enslaved native peoples have been the subject of controversy. Many states, cities and towns across the nation, including Baltimore, have grappled with the issue of what to do with the monuments that are perceived to glorify white racism.

The controversial statues have been a matter of debate in Baltimore for years. On June 30, 2015, Mayor Stephanie Rawlings Blake announced the creation of a special commission to review all of Baltimore's Confederate statues and historical assets. The committee consisted of four members from the Commission for Historical and Architectural Preservation and three members from the Baltimore City Public Arts Commission. Under the request, Mayor Blake directed the special commission to launch a conversation about each of the different Confederate monuments and other historical assets and make recommendations for their future in Baltimore. The mayor stated:

> *It is important that we recognize the delicate balance between respecting history and being offensive. I believe that by bringing together representatives from the art community and historians and gathering public testimony, we have a better chance of understanding the importance of historic monuments,*

not only the significance they have in our history but the role they should play in our future.[57]

Over the next six months, the commission conducted a thorough review of Confederate monuments on city-owned property, including gathering research and soliciting public testimony. It held four public meetings and heard comments from more than two hundred people. On August 16, 2016, the commission issued a series of recommendations to the mayor. The considered recommendations included preservation in place, the addition of new signage, relocation or removal.[58] On August 16, 2017, the city government removed the following four controversial monuments: Roger B. Taney Monument, Confederate Veterans Monument, Confederate Womens Monument and the Lee-Jackson Monument.

Another controversial monument, the Christopher Columbus Monument on Eastern Avenue and President Street, was destroyed by activists on July 4, 2020. The monument to John O'Donnell, also controversial because he owned enslaved people, was removed by the city government on April 5, 2021, following a petition from local community leaders and anti-racism groups.

In June 2022, Baltimore's Commission for Historical and Architectural Preservation announced that the city's four Confederate monuments would be transferred to the Geffen Museum of Contemporary Art in Los Angeles, California. The "Monuments" exhibit, set to open in the fall of 2023, will feature decommissioned Confederate monuments from cities across the country. According to the museum's executive director, Hamza Walker:

> *Baltimore's monuments touch on many different aspects of the national conversation surrounding Confederate monuments. Each is significant as an art object, having been made by prominent artists of the time and offer entry points to talk about historical memory, use of public space, and the Lost Cause. They are also significant because Baltimore is one of a handful of cities that removed their Confederate monuments following the "Unite the Right" rally in Charlottesville in 2017. It's an "exhibition to meet the moment" and will definitely be part of a national dialogue.*[59]

CHRISTOPHER COLUMBUS MONUMENT

Location: Eastern Avenue and President Street
Designers: Dolsiand and Simoncini
Erected: 1984

At one time, Baltimore had a fondness for Christopher Columbus (1451–1506), as there were once three monuments erected in his honor throughout the city. This statue of the famous explorer served as the focal point for Columbus Square, a landscaped plaza linking the city's Little Italy community with the Inner Harbor.

Efforts to obtain a statue of Columbus for the Little Italy community of Baltimore originated in the 1970s. The idea lay dormant until 1983, when the Italian American organization United of Maryland sought approval from city officials to move an existing statue from Druid Hill Park to the newly planned Columbus Square at Eastern Avenue and President Street. A dispute soon erupted between the Friends of Druid Hill Park, an organization dedicated to the preservation of the park, and the Italian American organization.

Representatives from both organizations debated the issue during a March 16, 1983 meeting of the board of park commissioners. The Druid Hill Park organization argued that the move would damage preservation efforts in the park and set a dangerous precedent for future groups that might want to "rape and pillage the park by relocating other statues." The group suggested that the Little Italy community commission a statue of its own rather than move one that had been in a city park for more than ninety years.[60] The protest had the desired effect, as a few weeks later, Mayor William Donald Schaefer announced that the Columbus statue would not be moved from Druid Hill Park.

Christopher Columbus Monument, Eastern Avenue and President Street. *Photo by author.*

When it became apparent that the Druid Hill Park statue would not be moved, the Italian American community began efforts to erect a new one. It established a nine-member Inner Harbor Columbus Statue Committee to oversee the project, including fundraising and construction. In late 1983, several members of the committee traveled to Carrara, Italy, where they commissioned sculptors Dolsiand and Simoncini to create the statue at a cost of $40,000.[61]

On October 18, 1984, an estimated crowd of six thousand people gathered on the east side of the Inner Harbor, just west of the Little Italy community, to witness the dedication of the Christopher Columbus statue. Mayor William Donald Schaefer presided over the ceremony. The president of the United States, Ronald Reagan, made a brief address and assisted Mayor Schaefer in the unveiling.[62]

As with other monuments honoring Christopher Columbus throughout the country, this statue has been embroiled in controversy. It is one of several historical monuments that have been toppled or removed amid protests demanding racial justice. In recent years, some historians and activists have sought to bring greater attention to the use of violence against native peoples and the involvement of Columbus in the slave trade. On July 4, 2020, protestors toppled the Columbus statue, broke it into pieces and tossed it into the harbor. The statue was subsequently recovered by city officials, but it was unable to be restored.

The marble statue surmounted a hexagonal base. It depicted Columbus facing east along Eastern Avenue into the rising sun, the direction from which he arrived in 1492. In his left hand, he held a rolled map, his right hand resting on a globe.

The inscriptions that were once inscribed on the pedestal read:

CHRISTOPHER COLUMBUS
DISCOVERER OF AMERICA
OCTOBER 12, 1492

DEDICATED TO THE
CITY OF BALTIMORE
BY THE
ITALIAN-AMERICAN
ORGANIZATION UNITED
OF MARYLAND
AND THE ITALIAN
AMERICAN COMMUNITY
OF BALTIMORE

OCTOBER 12, 1984
WILLIAM DONALD SCHAEFER, MAYOR

(This inscription was repeated on the back panel.)

Columbus's three ships were depicted in bas relief on separate panels. The inscriptions read:

> The Santa Maria
> 98 Feet Long and 27 Feet Wide
> Manned by 40 Men

> The Pinta
> 80 Feet Long and 20 Feet Wide
> Manned by 40 Men

> The Nina
> 66 Feet Wide and 20 Feet Wide
> Manned by 40 Men

Another panel depicted a harbor scene in Genoa, Italy. The inscription read:

> Genoa, Italy
> Birthplace of Columbus
> 1451

Another panel depicted Columbus in a rowboat with three sailors from his crew. The inscription read:

> The Landing in America
> October 12, 1492

Another panel depicted Columbus meeting with the indigenous people: The inscription read:

> Meeting with the Indians
> October 12, 1492

The inscription at the base of the monument read:

> Members of the Committee
> Dominic Averza—Police Commissioner Frank J. Battaglia—
> Senator Joseph Bonvegna

Councilman Dominic Mimi DiPietro—Albert J. Flora, Sr.—
Richard G. Francis
Frank M. Vallegia—Marco I. Palughi

CONFEDERATE VETERANS MONUMENT

Location: Mount Royal Avenue and Mosher Street
Designer: Frederick Ruckstuhl
Erected: 1903

This monument, titled *Glory Stands Beside Our Grief*, pays tribute to those Marylanders who served in the Confederate army and navy during the Civil War. It was presented to the city in 1903 by the Maryland Chapter, Daughters of the Confederacy.

In 1899, the organization sought to erect a monument commemorating the sacrifices made by the state's Confederate veterans and requested approval from the city government to place it in Druid Hill Park. The city council, in turn, passed a resolution granting their request, and it received the favorable endorsement of Mayor William Malster.[63] Frick's Triangle, a raised and enclosed space near the entrance to Druid Hill Park, was selected as a location, which was later changed to a square plot of land in the center of Mount Royal Avenue at Lanvale Street.[64]

A series of fundraisers was held to cover the cost. The last one, held in December 1902 atop the Richmond Market in the Old Fifth Regiment Armory, was a big social event. Members of the organization, selling handicrafts and gifts, raised more than $10,000.[65] After enough money had been raised, prominent sculptors were invited to submit designs. Frederick Wellington Ruckstuhl, director of sculpture for the St. Louis World's Fair, submitted the winning entry.

On May 2, 1903, a crowd of thousands gathered to witness the dedication of the Confederate Veterans Monument. Earlier that day, men from the Confederate Veterans Home in Pikesville assembled in Mount Vernon Place. The ceremonies began when the veterans, dressed in gray coats, led by Major General Andrew Trippe of the United Confederate Veterans, paraded to the monument site. Confederate flags appeared everywhere, and southern melodies were played as the crowd gathered. The Maryland Daughters of the Confederacy and invited guests occupied a large stand facing the monument.

Confederate Veterans Monument, Mount Royal Avenue and Mosher Street. *Photo by author.*

A wave of enthusiasm erupted as the line of veterans, carrying the old battle flags, reached the site. The bands played "Dixie," after which the crowd sang the hymn "Praise God from Whom All Blessings Flow." Reverend William Dame, chaplain of the Maryland Daughters of the Confederacy, gave an invocation.

The unveiling of the monument was performed by Margaret Lloyd Trimble, great-granddaughter of Major Isaac Trimble, and Nannie Young Hardcastle, great-granddaughter of Admiral Franklin Buchanan, who commanded the ironclad CSS *Virginia*. Simultaneously, the band played a rendition of "Tenting on the Old Campground" and "Maryland, My Maryland." Several wreaths and flowers were placed at the base by several United Daughters of the Confederacy members.

Captain Henry Howard delivered the main address. Captain G.W. Booth, the first vice-president of the Society of the Army and Navy of the Confederate States in Maryland, presented the monument to Mayor Thomas Hayes, who accepted it on behalf of the city.[66]

The bronze sculpture, cast at the Henry Bonnard Company of Founders, New York, rises to a height of approximately fourteen feet. It depicts a mortally wounded Confederate flag bearer being supported by a winged angel, who holds a wreath in her outstretched hand. The grouping surmounted an eight-foot-high pedestal of polished red granite:

[FRONT]	[BACK]	[RIGHT SIDE]	[LEFT SIDE]
GLORIUS VICTIS	GLORY	DEO VINDICI	FATTI MASCII
TO THE	STANDS BESIDE		PAROLE FEMINE
SOLDIERS AND	OUR GRIEF		
SAILORS			
OF MARYLAND	ERECTED BY		
IN THE SERVICE	THE MARYLAND		
OF THE	DAUGHTERS		
CONFEDERATE	OF THE		
STATES	CONFEDERACY		
OF AMERICA	FEBRUARY 1903		
1861–1865			

Amid the controversy surrounding Baltimore's Confederate monuments, the Confederate Veterans Monument was removed on August 16, 2017, by order of the mayor and city council.

CONFEDERATE WOMEN'S MONUMENT

Location: University Parkway and North Charles Street
Designers: J. Maxwell Miller, William G. Beecher, Frederick Law Olmsted
Erected: 1918

In 1911, the Maryland Chapter of the Daughters of the Confederacy, encouraged by the United Confederate Veterans of Maryland, resolved at its annual meeting to erect a monument in Baltimore "to the noble women of our city and state who were devoted to the Confederate cause."[67] To cover the cost of the monument, the women held various fundraising events such as tea parties, luncheons and bazaars. The state government aided the cause with a $12,000 contribution and appointed a five-member committee to oversee the project.[68]

The committee invited four prominent sculptors to submit designs: J. Maxwell Miller of Baltimore, Hans Schuler of Baltimore, Frederick W. Ruckstuhl of New York and Ernest W. Keyser of New York. After much deliberation, the commission was awarded to J. Maxwell Miller at a cost of $20,000.

A triangular plot of land at the intersection of University Parkway and North Charles Streets was selected as a location. Maxwell's design and the location received the approval of both the municipal art commission and the board of park commissioners.[69]

Dedication of the Confederate Women's Monument occurred on November 2, 1918, attended by a crowd of several hundred people. Reverend William Dane, rector of Memorial Protestant Episcopal Church and former Confederate chaplain, delivered the invocation. The main address was given by Judge James Trippe. Several musical selections were played throughout the exercises, starting with "The Star-Spangled Banner" and including "Dixie," "Maryland, My Maryland" and the "Bonnie Blue Flag."

Confederate Women's Monument, University Parkway and North Charles Street. *Photo by author.*

The monument, covered with both the national and Confederate flags, was unveiled by Mary Ringgold Trippe, granddaughter of the late General Andrew C. Trippe. The ceremony concluded with Reverend Eugene Connelly pronouncing the benediction.[70]

The monument consists of three figures, wrought in bronze, supported on a pedestal of polished red Missouri granite. The grouping depicts a flag-clutching Confederate soldier, wounded and being supported in the arms of a female nurse. Directly behind the pair stands a young woman, looking forward and clenching her hands together. The statue grouping is twelve feet in height, as is the pedestal. The base consisted of three granite steps. The architectural features are the work of William Gordon Beecher. The setting was laid out according to a plan by Frederick Law Olmsted.

The inscriptions on the pedestal read:

[FRONT]
TO THE
CONFEDERATE WOMEN
OF MARYLAND
1861–1865
THE BRAVE AT HOME

[BACK]
IN DIFFICULTY AND
DANGER
REGARDLESS OF SELF
THEY FED THE HUNGRY
CLOTHED THE NEEDY
NURSED THE WOUNDED
AND COMFORTED THE
DYING

Amid the controversy surrounding Baltimore's Confederate monuments, the Confederate Women's Monument was removed on August 16, 2017, by order of the mayor and city council.

ROBERT E. LEE–THOMAS "STONEWALL" JACKSON MONUMENT

Location: Wyman Park and Art Museum Drives
Designers: Laura Gardin Fraser, John Russell Pope
Erected: 1948

A seven-ton, double equestrian statue of two famous Confederate generals, Robert E. Lee (1807–1870) and Thomas "Stonewall" Jackson (1824–1863), once stood in Baltimore's Wyman Park. The statue was erected by wealthy Baltimore banker J. Henry Ferguson in 1948. When Ferguson died in 1934, he bequeathed $100,000 in his will to the Municipal Art Society of Baltimore to erect a monument representing the final parting of Generals Lee and Jackson just prior to the Battle of Chancellorsville on May 1, 1863.

The will stipulated that a committee be established to select a sculptor, choose a site and oversee construction. Ferguson's inspiration came from his admiration of the two generals, as expressed in his will: "They were my boyish heroes and mature judgement has only strengthened my admiration for them. They were great generals and Christian soldiers. They waged war like gentlemen, and I feel that their example should be held up for the youth of Maryland."[71]

In 1936, the Lee-Jackson Monument Committee held a national competition to choose a sculptor and selected Laura Gardin Fraser of South Carolina.[72] The contract covered the entire cost of the monument: statue, pedestal and foundation. Fraser retained the services of noted architect John Russell Pope to design the pedestal. Wyman Park and Art Museum Drives was selected as the location, which received the approval of the municipal art commission.[73]

Although started in 1936, it was not until 1948 that the monument was placed in Wyman Park. During the twelve-year period, there were many setbacks to overcome, starting with the 1936 Italian-Ethiopian War, which made it difficult for Fraser to obtain clay. This was followed by the entry of the United States into World War II, when the company commissioned to do the bronze work had to convert to military production. In addition, Fraser became ill, causing another delay. Finally, in October 1947, the statue arrived in Baltimore from Providence, Rhode Island, where it had been cast by the Gorham Company.

More than thirty thousand people attended the dedication of the Lee-Jackson Monument on May 1, 1948, including the grandchildren and other descendants of the two generals. A large parade starting at North Charles and 29th Streets and ending at the monument site preceded the event. The parade consisted of a color guard from the Maryland Army National Guard, cadets from the Virginia Military Institute and units of the regular army from Fort Meade.

George Radcliffe, president of the Maryland Historical Society, presided over the ceremony. The exercises started with an invocation by Reverend James E. Moore, pastor of the Mount Washington Presbyterian Church. This was followed by the playing of the national anthem by the Virginia

Robert E. Lee–Thomas "Stonewall" Jackson Monument, Wyman Park and Art Museum Drives. *Photo by author.*

Military Institute Band. Maryland governor William Preston Lane Jr. delivered a short speech, followed by a tribute to the donor J. Henry Ferguson by George Radcliffe.

Sculptor Laura Gardin Fraser was introduced to the crowd. Douglass Southall Freeman, a noted historian, delivered an address titled "The Great American Combat Team." Mayor Thomas D'Alesandro Jr. accepted the monument on behalf of the city, followed by the laying of a wreath by members of the United Daughters of the Confederacy.

The ceremony closed with a benediction by Right Reverend Noble C. Powell, bishop of the Protestant Episcopal Diocese of Maryland.[74]

The Lee-Jackson Monument depicts the final parting of Generals Lee and Jackson before the Battle of Chancellorsville. The foundation and pedestal were constructed of granite by the Stony Creek Memorial Corporation of Guilford, Connecticut. Sidney Waugh, president of the National Sculptor Society, said of the monument, "This monument is surely one of the most perfect in America."[75]

The inscription around the base of the pedestal read:

> The Parting of General Lee and Stonewall Jackson on the Eve of Chancellorsville
> They Were Great Generals and Christian Soldiers, and Waged War Like Gentlemen

The inscription around the top of the pedestal read:

> So Great Is My Confidence in General Lee that I Am Willing to Follow Him Blindfolded
> Straight as the Needle to the Pole Jackson Advanced to the Execution of My Purpose

Amid the controversy surrounding Baltimore's Confederate monuments, the Lee-Jackson Monument was removed on August 16, 2017, by order of the mayor and city council.

John O'Donnell Monument

Location: O'Donnell Street and Linwood Avenue
Designer: Tylden W. Street
Erected: 1980

In the historic waterfront neighborhood of Canton stood a monument to John O'Donnell (1749–1805), a famous seafarer and prominent Baltimore merchant. Located in Canton Square, the bronze statue was located on the site of O'Donnell's former estate, Canton, named after Canton, China, where O'Donnell established a lucrative trading business.

John O'Donnell Monument, O'Donnell Street and Linwood Avenue. *Photo by author.*

The monument to O'Donnell was the result of a collaborative effort between the Canton Improvement Association and the City of Baltimore. The sculptor, Tylden W. Streett of the Maryland Institute College of Art, donated his services. The $30,000 cost was paid by the Baltimore City government.[76]

Dedication of the John O'Donnell Monument occurred on April 12, 1980. The brief ceremony was attended by a small crowd, including the sculptor, members of the Canton Improvement Association and Mayor William Donald Schaefer.

The bronze statue of John O'Donnell is dressed in the clothing of an eighteenth-century gentleman, standing with his left arm outstretched. He is holding a hat in his right hand. The statue rested upon a large concrete pedestal.

The inscription on the pedestal read:

Captain John O'Donnell
1749–1805

The inscription on the bronze tablet embedded into the sidewalk in front of the pedestal read:

Captain John O'Donnell the founder of the
Canton Community was a man of great vision
and accomplishment. He initiated trade between
Canton, China and Baltimore in 1785 operating
his own merchant sailing vessels. This public
square, once the site of the Canton Market, is
dedicated in his honor.

The Canton Improvement Association
The Board of Recreation and Parks
The City of Baltimore
Mayor William Donald Schaefer

On April 5, 2021, the John O'Donnell statue was removed by the City
of Baltimore. The removal was the latest effort in a widespread movement
involving monuments that honored people with ties to America's racist
past. It came as the Canton Community Association was studying ways to
make the community more welcome and inclusive. An online petition to
remove the statue by the association and the Canton Anti-Racist Alliance
was signed by more than nine hundred people. Upon removal of the statue,
Mayor Brandon Scott issued a statement: "Tonight, the hostile vestige to
the notorious enslaver Captain John O'Donnell no longer stands in Canton
Square. This is a historical moment, however, countless publicly named
monuments…across Baltimore remain that must be reassessed."[77]

ROGER B. TANEY MONUMENT

Location: Mount Vernon Place
Designer: William Henry Rinehart
Erected: 1887

In 1887, a bronze likeness of the famous jurist, political leader and
Maryland native Roger Taney (1777–1864) was presented to the City of
Baltimore as a gift from successful businessman and art collector William
T. Walters.[78] The statue was a replica of a larger one that once stood on
the grounds of the statehouse in Annapolis, Maryland. William Henry
Rinehart, a well-known Maryland sculptor, created the statue after being
commissioned by the Maryland legislature in 1872.

Roger B. Taney Monument, Mount Vernon Place. *Photo by author.*

Taney served as chief justice of the U.S. Supreme Court from 1836 until his death in 1864. Many important decisions were handed down by the Taney court. None, however, had more of an impact on American history than did the decision for the famous Dred Scott case. Taney wrote the majority opinion, ruling that Black slaves were not citizens of the United States and therefore could not bring suit in federal court.

The larger-than-life size statue is approximately seven feet, seven inches in height. Taney is depicted in his judicial robes, seated in a cushioned chair. His left hand rests on a book, while his right hand rests on his lap, holding a scroll. The statue was cast in bronze by the Royal Foundry in Munich, Germany.

The inscription on a bronze tablet that was located on the base of the monument read:

ROGER B. TANEY
OF MARYLAND
CHIEF JUSTICE

In 2016, the Special Commission to Review Baltimore's Public Confederate Monuments recommended removing the Taney Monument. The decision was based on Taney's decision in the Dred Scott case, which advanced slavery in the United States and was tied to the Confederate cause. On August 16, 2017, the Taney Monument was removed on orders from the mayor and city council.

Chapter 5

EVENTS

Fallsway Monument

Location: Fallsway, Guilford Avenue and Biddle Street
Designers: Hans Schuler, Theodore Pietsch
Erected: 1915

In 1915, the city government erected this monument to commemorate completion of one of the most significant construction projects in the history of Baltimore, the Fallsway. The monument was designed by Baltimore architect Theodore Pietsch.[79] Situated in a parklike setting overlooking the Fallsway, it was constructed at a cost of $10,000 by the David M. Andrew Company of Baltimore.[80]

The Jones Falls was once a navigable river that carried boats as far north as Saratoga Street, but it later degenerated into an ugly, foul-smelling canal of water. The river became a constant source of dangerous floods until overlaid with masonry and converted into a major thoroughfare, the Fallsway. Work began on the project in 1911 and finished in late 1914. The reclaimed land established an important highway for the center of the business district.

With thousands of persons in attendance, city officials dedicated the Fallsway Monument on February 27, 1915. Dignitaries and invited guests occupied a small stand north of the monument, in front of which Steinwald's Band entertained the crowd. The ceremony lasted over one hour. Charles

Fallsway Monument, Fallsway, Guilford Avenue and Biddle Street. *Photo by author.*

England, chair of the Sewage Commission, delivered the opening remarks. Dr. Henry Barton Jacobs, a member of the Johns Hopkins Hospital Board of Trustees, served as master of ceremonies. Other speakers included Mayor James Preston; former mayor J. Barry Mahool; Francis K. Carey, first chairperson of the Committee on the City Plan; and Calvin W. Hendrick, chief engineer of the Sewage Commission. Mayor Preston unveiled the figure adorning the top, which had been covered by an American flag.[81]

Although the fountain is no longer functioning, it has a small trough at its base from which dogs could drink. Above these are troughs for the watering of horses and fountains from which people could drink. Engraved on the four sides of the column, which is about ten feet in height, are the names of the members of the various city boards and commissions that played a role in the Fallsway Project, along with the city seal. Granite benches occupy each side of the monument. The pedestal, with its colonnades and festooned urns, is symbolic of its purpose. Adorning the top of the column is a figure of a woman, created by sculptor Hans Schuler, seven feet in height, seated on a rock. She holds an urn in her left hand, from which water is flowing. She holds myrtle and the city shield in her right hand.

The inscriptions on the sides read:

[Front]
The
Fallsway
Completed
December 1914
James H. Preston
Mayor
Calvin W. Henrick
Engineer

[Back]
Commissioners
for
Opening Streets
Eugene E. Grannan

President
John L. Sanford
Henry A. Remley
Commission
on
City Plan
Francis K. Carey
Chairman
1909–1911
Josias Pennington
Chairman
George S. Jackson
Calvin W. Henrick
William B. Hurst
Joseph W. Shirley
W.W. Emmart
Herbert H. Sheridan
James H. Preston

Jones Falls Improvement began August 7, 1911.
Completed December 1914. Street bridges eliminated

10, railroad bridges 3, land redeemed about 600,000
square feet creating a new 75-foot driveway
from Mount Royal Avenue to Baltimore Street
and Market Place, a distance of 6677 feet

[Left Side]
Board
of
Estimates
James H. Preston
Mayor
John Hubert
President
Samuel S. Field
City Solicitor
H. Kent McKay
City Engineer
Contractors
Mortimer M. Elkan
Fisher and Carozza
Claiborne Johnson Co.
David M. Andrews Co.

Hans Schuler
Sculptor

[Right Side]
Sewage
Commission
City of Baltimore
Charles England
Chairman
James H. Preston
Mayor Ex-Officio
Morris Whitridge
Ira Remson
William B. Kines
Gustav Siegmund
Thomas J. Shrycock

E. Clay Timanus
Mayor
1905–1907
J. Barry Mahool
Mayor
1907–1911
Brig. Gen. Peter Leary, Jr.
Chairman
1905–1913
William D. Pratt
1905–1913
J. Edward Mohler
1905–1912
William W. McIntire
1911–1912
Calvin W. Henrick
Alfred H. Hartman
Div. Engineer
W.A. Megraw, Dsg. Engr.
C.K. Allen, Asst. Ngr.

HOLOCAUST MEMORIAL

Location: Gay and Water Streets
Designers: Donald Kann, Athur Valk
Erected: 1980

Baltimore's Holocaust Memorial has a twofold purpose: to commemorate the lives of 6 million European Jews who were systematically murdered by the Nazis between 1933 and 1945 and to be a constant reminder that the tragedy of the Holocaust must never be repeated. When it was erected in 1980, Baltimore became one of a few American cities with a formal Holocaust memorial.

A memorial in downtown Baltimore to the victims of the Holocaust was first proposed in 1968 by Alvin D. Fisher, a teacher from Owings Mills, Maryland. Fisher shared his vision of a "living memorial" with leaders of the city's Jewish community and suggested the planting of six hundred flowering trees, one for each ten thousand victims of the Holocaust. In 1970, the Baltimore Jewish Council appointed him chairman of a committee whose members were asked to recommend "some kind of suitable memorial to the six million Jews." In 1976, after years of discussing various ideas, the committee decided on the tree planting proposal. As a location, the Baltimore Jewish Council selected the harbor campus of the Community College of Baltimore. The one-acre parcel of land—bounded by Gay, Water and Lombard Streets—was donated by the college trustees.[82]

In August 1978, the Baltimore Jewish Council held a design competition, of which the guidelines called for the preservation of "green and open space" with the planting of trees and a physical structure that would inspire "dignified respect for the six million." Of the ten entries submitted, the winning design was a collaborative effort by Baltimore architect Donald Kann and local urban designer Arthur Valk.[83]

On October 13, 1978, the Charles Center–Inner Harbor Development Corporation, a quasi-government organization responsible for the development of the city's downtown area, subsequently approved the design, being "impressed by the quality of the new proposal," calling it "an eloquent and fitting symbol…of the highest order."[84] Later that fall, the Baltimore Jewish Council committed its resources to the project and established the Holocaust Memorial Fund to raise the necessary funds. The $300,000 cost was covered by contributions from many organizations, businesses and individuals.

On April 22, 1979, Yom HaShoah, or Holocaust Remembrance Day, more than five hundred people gathered for a groundbreaking ceremony. Addresses were delivered by Rabbi Donald Berlin and Ronald Shapiro of the Baltimore Jewish Council. Mayor William Donald Schaefer commended the Jewish community for establishing the memorial "in an area where the city is coming to life again." The principal speaker was Holocaust scholar Alan Udoff.

Symbolic of the occasion was the lighting of twelve candles by twelve Holocaust survivors. The one-hour ceremony concluded with a prayer by Rabbi Nahum Ben-Natan.[85]

After its completion, the Baltimore Jewish Council presented the Holocaust Memorial to the city with a solemn ceremony on November 2, 1980. The main speaker was Rabbi Herbert A. Friedman, a former United Jewish Appeal official who assisted survivors of the Holocaust. Others participating in the ceremony included Mayor William Donald Schaefer; City Councilman Kweisi Mfume; Rabbi Seymour Essrog, president of the Baltimore Jewish Council; Charles Tildon Jr., chairman of the Community College of Baltimore Board of Trustees; Richard Manekin, chairman of the

Holocaust Memorial, Gay and Water Streets. *Photo by author.*

Holocaust Memorial Fund Board; Cantor Abraham Denberg of the Beth Tfiloh Congregation; and Rabbi Donald Berlin, chairman of the Holocaust Activities Committee.[86]

The memorial is a combination of symbolic architecture and landscaping, consisting of a concrete memorial facing the plaza on the north side and a parklike setting of trees on the south. It was designed so that each aspect of the memorial would evoke sensations symbolic of the Holocaust experience. Two huge monoliths eighty feet by ninety feet of cantilevered bleached gray blocks—which were deliberately featureless, cold and brutal—represent the brutality of the Nazi machine.

On the wall is a granite inscription consecrating the memorial to the victims of the Holocaust and listing the thirty-nine concentration camps where they died. The stark structures are disfigured in a calculated way, scored with lines and drilled with holes, to remind the viewer of how systematically the destruction of people was planned. The sense of pressure and darkness increases as one walks under or between the monoliths.

In coming to the open space beyond the structures, the viewer, still surrounded by the concrete memorial, enters an area of light. The light represents the hope of man for a better future despite the forces of evil that surround him. The viewer then faces a wall on which the inscription has been engraved. Here, the explicit purpose of the memorial, consecration and remembrance are stated with the names of the thirty-nine death camps in which the victims of the Holocaust were murdered. On the south side of the memorial, six rows of early blooming pear trees can be found in the parklike setting representing the 6 million Jews who were murdered. The trees bloom every spring, symbolizing once again man's yearning for a world of peace and tolerance.

The inscription on the memorial reads:

> We consecrate this memorial to the six million Jews murdered by the Nazis in Europe, 1933–1945, in the Holocaust. Six million victims, including more than one million children, were martyred solely because they were Jews. We remember and shall not forget the genocide which the mind cannot imagine: the degradation, the starvation, the torture, the rape, the experimentation on humans, the gassings, the burnings, the mass executions, we remember and shall not forget the concentration camps, monuments of man's capacity for evil, where Jews suffered and died. We remember and shall not forget the heroic resistance of the Jews in the cities, the ghettos, the forests, and in the very death camps themselves. We remember and shall not forget the righteous of all faiths who risked their lives to save Jews. We remember and shall not forget the world's silence and indifference which led not only to the Holocaust but to the deaths of millions of other people.

> The People of Baltimore
> November 1980

In 1987, two Baltimore businessmen, Melvin M. Berger and Jack Luskin, commissioned Maryland-born and internationally renowned artist Joseph Sheppard to create a sculpture to supplement the Holocaust memorial. It serves as a grim reminder of the Holocaust and a deterrent to any recurrence of it again. Sheppard always had intense feelings about the Holocaust after having heard, read and studied photographs of the horror. Soon after receiving his commission, Sheppard visited the Dachau

Concentration Camp, and upon returning to his studio in Italy, he created the sculpture.

Dedication occurred on November 6, 1988, three days short of the fiftieth anniversary of *Kristallnacht*, or "Night of Broken Glass." On that night, November 9, 1938, Jewish shops and synagogues throughout Germany were destroyed, and more than thirty thousand Jews were arrested and sent to concentration camps.

The sculpture represents the flame of death that offered the only escape from suffering for the Holocaust victims. In the flame is depicted the images particular to the tragedy—old and young, male and female, starved, broken and naked. The total height of the sculpture is sixteen feet, including the pedestal.

The inscription on the pedestal reads:

> "Those Who Cannot Remember the Past Are Condemned to Repeat It"
> George Santayana 1863–1952

> A Gift of Rememrance
> Jeanne and Melvin Berger
> Jean and Jack Luskin
> Sculptor, Joseph Sheppard 1930–

Katyn Memorial

Location: President and Aliceanna Streets
Designer: Andrzej Pitsynski
Erected: 2000

Located in historic Fells Point, where many Polish immigrants received their first glimpse of America, Baltimoreans of Polish descent erected this memorial in honor of the fifteen thousand Polish army officers who were massacred in the Katyn Forest by the Soviet Union in 1940. The bronze sculpture has the distinction of being the tallest in the city, as well as the largest one on the East Coast.

The origins of the National Katyn Memorial began with Major Clement A. Knefel, who learned of the massacre when he was stationed in Germany during the Nuremberg trials of Nazi leaders following World War II. After

Katyn Memorial,
President and
Aliceanna Streets.
Photo by author.

returning to the United States, he began collecting funds for a memorial to honor the victims of the tragedy. Appealing mostly to veterans organizations, he managed to raise $1,600 over ten years. In 1989, Major Knefel appealed to the Maryland Division of the Polish American Congress. The organization approved the idea to erect a memorial and formed the Katyn Memorial Committee, with Clement Knefel as chairperson.

Support came from beyond the Polish American community. Honorary chairpersons included Mayor Kurt Schmoke, former Maryland governor William Donald Schaefer, U.S. Senators Barbara Mikulski and Paul Sarbanes and city council president Mary Pat Clark. The largest donation of $36,500 came from the Associated Jewish Community Federation of Baltimore. Over time, $1.4 million was collected.

In early 1994, the Katyn Memorial Committee, based on the recommendation of the Polish embassy, commissioned Andrzej Pitsynski, a Polish-born sculptor from New Jersey, to design and create the memorial.

Although the city council formally designated the site for the memorial, the five-member municipal art commission withheld its required approval of Pitsynski's design. The commission believed "that the spirit and intent of the memorial would be better served with a design that is more figurative or representational…and the proposed size of the memorial was 'too large for the surroundings.'"[87]

The Katyn Memorial Committee appealed the decision to Mayor Kurt Schmoke, who was in favor of the design and interceded in the matter. In doing so, the design was subsequently approved by the municipal art commission.[88] The sculpture was completed in the summer of 2000 and arrived in Baltimore that September.

Dedication of the Katyn Memorial occurred on November 19, 2000, attended by a crowd of more than five hundred people, including diplomats from eastern Europe. The committee chair, Alfred Wisniewski, was so overcome with emotion that he could not speak during the ceremonies. He had his brother, Stanislaus, read a statement. A contingent of military reenactors, dressed in World War II–era Polish uniforms, marched past the stage. The Three Hundred Eighty-Ninth Army Band played traditional Polish patriotic songs.

The main speaker for the ceremony was U.S. Senator Barbara Mikulski. At the end of the two-hour ceremony, the sculptor Andrzej Pitsynski and Alfred Wisniewski climbed into a cherry picker and placed a small container of soil from the Katyn Forest on the sculpture. The ceremony concluded with a priest blessing the memorial followed by a bugler playing taps.[89]

Soaring forty-four feet above a traffic circle, the bronze sculpture weighs approximately twelve tons. Standing atop a mountain whose waters run over black granite bricks, it depicts soldiers against flames that are gilded in gold leaf. World War II–era soldiers are depicted alongside other great warrior heroes from Poland's history. The flames include a cut-out in the shape of an eagle, the symbol of Poland.

The inscription on the base of the memorial reads:

KATYN, 1940

MARYLAND 9/11 MEMORIAL

Location: World Trade Center Plaza
Designer: Zigler and Snead, Architects
Erected: 2011

A key feature of Baltimore's World Trade Center Plaza, the Maryland 9/11 Memorial, honors the sixty-three Marylanders who lost their lives during the terrorist attack of September 11, 2001. On that day, nineteen terrorists hijacked four commercial airplanes. They intentionally flew two of the planes into the Twin Towers of the World Trade Center in New York City and a third plane into the Pentagon in Washington, D.C. Learning about the other hijackings, passengers and crew members aboard the fourth plane forced the hijacking pilot to crash the plane into a Pennsylvania field. More than three thousand people were killed on that day, the single largest loss of life from a foreign attack on American soil. The memorial is a tribute to the extraordinary heroism and sacrifice of the victims, rescuers, first responders and their families.

After the events of that horrific day, the Maryland 9/11 Memorial Advisory Committee was established to oversee construction of a memorial to honor those lives lost. After a national search by the committee, the Baltimore architectural firm of Zigler and Snead was selected to lead the design team. Zigler and Snead worked with landscape architects Mahan Rykiel Associates and engineering firms Robert Silman and Associates to create the memorial. The $2 million cost was funded by private and public donations.

Dedicated on September 11, 2011, the tenth anniversary of the attack, the memorial stands as a stark reminder of one of the nation's darkest days. The ceremony was attended by people who lost family members on that day and government officials, including Senator Barbara Mikulski.[90]

Maryland 9/11 Memorial, World Trade Center Plaza. *Photo by author.*

The focal point of the memorial is an artifact from the Twin Towers, selected by a delegation of the Maryland Commission on Public Art, the Maryland Port Administration and the Maryland State Arts Council. The twenty-two-foot-long steel artifact consists of three twisted and torn amalgamated steel columns. Three limestone artifacts from the Pentagon and a large black granite monolith representing those lost in the Pennsylvania crash are featured in the design. The names and birthdays of the sixty-three Marylanders lost in the attack are inscribed on the base.

PRIDE OF BALTIMORE MEMORIAL

Location: Rash Field and Key Highway
Designer: Dave Jenkins
Erected: 1988

This somber memorial, in the form of a ship's foremast, pays tribute to the four crew members from the clipper ship *Pride of Baltimore* who lost their lives when the ship was lost at sea in a terrible storm on May 14, 1986.

The *Pride* sailed the seas for eleven years as "Baltimore's Goodwill Ambassador." It was commissioned by the city of Baltimore and constructed using the same shipbuilding techniques that built the original Baltimore clippers of the early nineteenth century.[91] It was heading home to Baltimore on the last leg of a successful European voyage when it sank in a freak storm. The *Pride*'s captain and three other crew members perished in the tragedy.

In October 1986, the *Pride of Baltimore*'s board of directors held a design competition to find a suitable memorial that would honor the ill-fated ship and its lost crew members. The original winning entry was a bronze statue of a sailor taking a sighting through a sextant. The board rejected the design, however, in favor of the current one by Dave Jenkins, a former *Pride of Baltimore* crew member. Construction of the memorial began in March 1988.

The Pride of Baltimore Memorial was dedicated on May 14, 1988, the second anniversary of the disaster. A crowd of about one hundred people gathered for the ceremony, including former crew members and builders. Speakers included William Beasman, chairman of the board of the *Pride of Baltimore*, and Maryland congresswoman Helen Delich Bentley.[92]

Pride of Baltimore Memorial, Rash Field and Key Highway. *Photo by author.*

The memorial consists of a ninety-foot replica of the *Pride*'s foremast into a foundation of red Texas granite. This is bordered on the east and west sides by large granite blocks, also of red Texas granite. The blocks measure approximately fifteen feet by six feet and are about four feet in height. They are engraved with dedicatory inscriptions. There is also a block made of red Texas granite at the north entrance to the memorial with a bronze image of the ship mounted onto it and a dedicatory inscription.

The inscriptions on the granite block bordering the foundation reads:

[WEST SIDE]
PRIDE OF BALTIMORE
LOST AT SEA
MAY 14, 1986

Captain Armin Elsaessser, III Nina Schack
Barry Duckworth Vincent Lazzaro

[East Side]
I Saw Her, Her Sails Were Blowing, Her Flags Were Waving
She Turned Slowly and Headed to Ports Unknown. If You Look
Real Hard Right Now You Can See Her Rounding the Bend, Sails
Filled, Her Cannons Firing a Final Salute. Let the Pride
Sail On. Sail On in Her Memory. Let the Pride Sail On
Till the Sunset of Our Memories.

William Donald Schaefer
Mayor of Baltimore
June 1, 1986

What Lies Ahead Is Unknown—A Source of Mystery and
Apprehension. Perhaps the Allure of the Sailing Life
Always Moving, Always Changing, Always Wondering What the
Next Passage Will Be—Like and What We Will Discover at the
Other End.

This Time Our Destination Is Home—the Chesapeake Bay and
Baltimore. It Is Always a Relief for the Captain, and I
Suspect the Ship, to Have Our Lines Ashore and Fast Where
Pride Is Safest—the Fingers Piers at the Inner Harbor.

Captain Armin E. Elsaesser, III
Pride's Log
May 7, 1986

The inscription on the granite block at the north entrance to the memorial
reads:

On May 14, 1986, the Pride of Baltimore
Her Captain, and Three Members of Her
Crew Were Lost at Sea

The Pride Now Rests at the End of a Goodwill
Journey that Covered 150,000 Miles and
Touched 125 Cities Around the World

Yet Her Precious Cargo—the Spirit of the
People Who Sent Her Forth and of Those Who
Received Her—Will Never Be Lost

SCHOOL CHILDREN'S MEMORIAL TO "THE STAR-SPANGLED BANNER"

Location: Patterson Park, Patterson Park Avenue and Pratt Street
Designer: J. Maxwell Miller
Erected: 1914

In May 1914, the National Star-Spangled Banner Centennial Commission made a request to Baltimore's school board asking that the children collect money for a memorial commemorating the 100th anniversary of the writing of "The Star-Spangled Banner."[93] Designed by local artist J. Maxwell Miller, this memorial is the result of that request.

Dedication of the School Children's Memorial to the Star-Spangled Banner took place in Baltimore's Patterson Park on September 11, 1914, with three thousand people in attendance. The memorial stood as a centerpiece on a float in the Star-Spangled Banner centennial parade through the city. Mayor James H. Preston, the board of school commissioners and

School Children's Memorial to "The Star-Spangled Banner," Patterson Park Avenue and Pratt Street. *Photo by author.*

other officials attended the exercises, which were presided over by school commissioner James Delevett. Reverend Dr. M. Lichilter, pastor of Grace Methodist Episcopal Church, opened the ceremony with a prayer.

Marjorie and Celeste Key, the great-grandnieces of Francis Scott Key, unveiled the memorial, after which Mayor Preston accepted it on behalf of the city and gave a short address. An address was also made by Judge Henry Stockbridge of the Maryland Court of Appeals and Assistant School Superintendent Charles J. Koch.[94]

The memorial, cast in bronze, depicts a schoolboy and schoolgirl with a slate and books, holding an unfurled scroll between them. A dedicatory inscription is shown on the scroll. The base is a boulder three feet in height with oak leaves in the background.

The inscription on the bronze scroll reads:

> TO COMMEMORATE THE CENTENNIAL OF THE WRITING
> OF THE STAR-SPANGLED BANNER, THE PUPILS OF
> THE PUBLIC SCHOOLS OF BALTIMORE HAVE ERECTED
> THIS MEMORIAL UPON HAMPSTEAD HILL, WHERE IN
> SEPTEMBER 1814 THE CITIZEN SOLDIERS
> OF MARYLAND STOOD READY TO SACRIFICE THEIR
> LIVES IN DEFENSE OF THEIR HOMES AND THEIR
> COUNTRY
> 1914

Chapter 6

GOVERNMENT OFFICIALS

CECIL CALVERT MONUMENT

Location: Saint Paul and Lexington Streets
Designer: Albert Weinert
Erected: 1908

This bronze statue of Cecil Calvert (1605–1675), the second Lord Baltimore and First Proprietor of Maryland, stands at the west entrance of Baltimore's Clarence M. Mitchell Jr. Courthouse. As Maryland's first governor, Calvert instituted freedom of worship, separation of church and state and the right of free men to participate in the lawmaking process.

In 1906, the Society of Colonial Wars in Maryland made known its intention to erect a statue of Cecil Calvert by New York sculptor Albert Weinert in Battle Monument Plaza.[95] After obtaining its goal of $5,000 by popular subscription, the society asked the city government to donate the pedestal, and an ordinance appropriating $5,000 for the pedestal was subsequently introduced and approved by the city council.[96]

In a unanimous decision, the municipal art commission rejected the Battle Monument Plaza location, citing that it was "not the place for the statue as presented in the design." The commission believed that the statue "was not of sufficient height for such a broad place."[97] Based on the adverse report from the art commission, the city government disapproved the $5,000

Cecil Calvert Monument, Clarence M. Mitchell Jr. Courthouse entrance, Saint Paul and Lexington Streets. *Photo by author.*

expenditure for the pedestal.[98] As an alternative site, the Society of Colonial Wars in Maryland was offered the west side steps of the courthouse, which did receive the approval of the municipal art commission.[99]

The new location was not without controversy either, as it was approved over the objections of several city council members and court officials. Council member George Konig argued that "the beauty of the west façade of the courthouse would be greatly marred were the statue placed on the steps."[100] State's Attorney Albert Owens claimed that the courthouse would not be improved by the addition of "what may be relatively classified as a piece of bric-a-brac."[101] On March 23, 1908, a bill was introduced in the city council approving the courthouse site for the statue and appropriating $2,100 for its pedestal.[102] The bill was approved and endorsed by Mayor Mahool.

On November 21, 1908, more than two thousand people attended the dedication ceremony of the Cecil Calvert Monument, including Governor Austin Crothers, Mayor Mahool, members of the city council and officers of the Society of Colonial Wars in Maryland. Led by the Fifth Regiment

Army Band, detachments from the Fourth and Fifth Regiments paraded down Charles Street to Lexington and east to the courthouse.

The band played "America" as members of the official party occupied their seats on the platform around the statue. Governor Crothers presided over the exercises and gave the opening address. DeCourcy W. Thom, governor of the Society of Colonial Wars in Maryland, delivered the main address. Joseph Lancaster Brent, a descendant of Cecil Calvert, unveiled the statue, which was covered by the national and state flags. The unveiling was followed by a rendition of "Maryland, My Maryland" by the band and the acceptance of the statue by Mayor Mahool. The exercises concluded with the playing of "The Star-Spangled Banner."[103]

The statue, which stands eight feet, six inches in height, was cast in New York by the Roman Bronze Works Company. The marble pedestal that supports the statue is six feet, nine inches in height and was designed by Howard Sill of Baltimore. Calvert is dressed in the clothing of a seventeenth-century gentleman, with hair of long flowing curls and wearing a wide-brimmed hat. He is standing and holding the Maryland Charter in his left hand, while his right hand leans on a sword. The Calvert family coat of arms appears on the front of the pedestal.

The inscription on the front of the pedestal reads:

CECILIUS CALVERT
1606–1675
FOUNDER OF MARYLAND

ERECTED UNDER THE AUSPICES OF THE SOCIETY
OF COLONIAL WARS IN THE STATE OF MARYLAND
NOVEMBER 21, 1908, DECOURCY WRIGHT THOM
GOVERNOR OF THE SOCIETY

The inscription on the back of the pedestal reads:

Cecilius Calvert, Baron Baltimore
of Baltimore in the kingdom
Ireland, absolute lord and proprietary
of the province of Maryland and
Avalon in America. Who on November
13, 1663, with the cooperation and
assent of the first colonists proclaimed

in England, and on March 25, 1634,
established in the palatinate of Maryland
for the first time in the English
speaking world freedom of religious
worship according to any Christian
form and separation of the church and
state

THOMAS D'ALESANDRO JR. MEMORIAL

Location: Charles Center Plaza, Charles and Lexington Streets
Designer: Lloyd Lillie
Erected: 1987

Located in Charles Center Plaza, where Baltimore's downtown renaissance began, stands two larger-than-life statues of one of the city's most respected mayors, Thomas D'Alesandro Jr. (1903–1987). It was through his determination and leadership that Baltimore inaugurated its successful urban renewal program.

In May 1980, Mayor William Donald Schaefer expressed a desire to have the former mayor's contributions recognized in some permanent way in Charles Center Plaza. The mayor formed a committee of government, business and civic leaders whose task it was to recommend and oversee a suitable memorial for the former mayor. Chaired by city attorney Eugene M. Feinblatt, the committee discussed several ideas and decided on the installation of a memorial clock. The clock would serve the dual functions of being a point of interest as well as a utilitarian object in the urban environment.

Mayor Schaefer and Eugene Feinblatt discussed the idea of engaging a distinguished Italian sculptor or architect to design the pedestal and clock face. In December 1981, after investigating and seeking advice about working architects in Italy, the committee selected Also Rossi. Plans were eventually dropped, however, after Rossi submitted his $50,000 estimate, the cost being more than could be raised. As an alternative, the committee decided to erect a representative sculpture and, in July 1983, obtained the services of Lloyd Lillie, an artist on the faculty of Boston University.

During a city hall press conference on December 10, 1985, with former mayor Thomas D'Alesandro Jr. in attendance, Mayor Schaefer unveiled photographs of two scale models. One depicted D'Alesandro standing and

Thomas D'Alesandro Jr. Memorial, Charles Center Plaza, Charles and Lexington Streets. *Photo by author.*

leaning on a railing. The other showed him seated and relaxing on a bench. The former mayor, upon seeing the models, remarked, "You have made it possible for me to smell my flowers ahead of time." Lillie decided to create two sculptures to show different sides of the subject. Lillie stated, "The figure on the railing would be the early part of D'Alesandro's career…and the other seated figure would be the man who was always available to the people."[104]

Dedication of the Thomas D'Alesandro Jr. Memorial occurred on March 25, 1987. Mayor Clarence "Du" Burns—along with former mayors J. Harold Grady, Thomas D'Alesandro III and William Donald Schaefer—joined the former mayor for the unveiling of his statues.[105]

The inscription on a bronze tablet embedded into the sidewalk between the two statues reads:

> IN HONOR OF
> MAYOR THOMAS D'ALESANDRO, JR.
> UNDER WHOSE LEADERSHIP
> THE CHARLES CENTER PROJECT
> WAS UNDERTAKEN
> 1958
> BY HIS FRIENDS AND
> THE CITIZENS OF BALTIMORE

FERDINAND LATROBE MONUMENT

Location: Broadway and East Baltimore Street
Designer: J. Maxwell Miller and Edward Berge, sculptors; W. Gordon
Beecher, architect
Erected: 1914

The Baltimore city government erected this monument in honor of seven-term mayor Ferdinand Latrobe (1833–1911). A lawyer and financier, Latrobe was mayor for a total of thirteen years during a twenty-year period, making him one of the city's longest-serving mayors. He was a popular mayor whose many improvements and reforms left an enduring impact on the city.

In 1913, two years after Latrobe's death, the mayor and city council approved an ordinance appropriating $5,000 for the erection of a monument in his honor. The legislation also provided for the establishment of a commission to select a location and a sculptor and oversee construction of the monument.[106] The Latrobe Monument Commission selected local sculptors Edward Berge and J. Maxwell Miller and architect W. Gordon Beecher to perform the work at a cost of $4,800. As a location, the commission selected a plot of ground on Broadway, just north of East Baltimore Street.[107]

Dedication of the Ferdinand Latrobe Monument occurred on June 1, 1914, with thousands of citizens in attendance, including relatives and friends of the former mayor. Virginia Latrobe released the large American flag that covered the statue of her father. Members of the city council laid a wreath at the base. The Latrobe Monument Commission presented it to Mayor James Preston, who received it on behalf of the citizens of Baltimore. The main address was delivered by A.S. Goldsborough, secretary of the Factory Site Commission. An invocation was given by Reverend Dr. Hugh Birckhead, pastor of Emmanuel Protestant Episcopal Church. The ceremony closed with a benediction by Monsignor George Devine of St. John's Catholic Church.[108]

The Ferdinand Latrobe Monument consists of a granite pedestal on which stands a bronze statue of Latrobe, nine feet in height. Latrobe is standing in front of a chair, also of bronze. Directly behind the chair is a large granite pier, around whose top can be found seven bronze wreaths. Within each wreath is inscribed the date of each mayoral election. On the front of the pedestal there is a replica of the city seal.

The dates inscribed inside the wreaths surrounding the pier include:

1875 1878 1879 1883 1887 1891 1893

Ferdinand Latrobe Monument, Broadway and East Baltimore Street. *Photo by author.*

The inscription on the back of the pedestal reads:

FERDINAND CLAIBORNE LATROBE
1833–1911

SEVEN TIMES MAYOR OF BALTIMORE
IN GRATEFUL ACKNOWLEDGMENT
OF HIS EMINENT SERVICES TO THE
CITY HAS ERECTED THIS MONUMENT

Commission
James H. Preston, Mayor
Michael Jenkins
Frank A. Furst
John M. Carter
Frank N. Hoen

Cast at the Roman Bronze Works, NY
Edward Berge, J. Maxwell Miller, sculptors
W.G. Beecher, arch.

THURGOOD MARSHALL MONUMENT

Location: Pratt Street and Hopkins Place
Designer: Reuben Kramer
Erected: 1980

Located in front of the federal courthouse in Baltimore stands a monument in honor of Thurgood Marshall (1908–1993), a Baltimore native, civil rights activist and first African American justice on the U.S. Supreme Court. Prior to his judicial service, Marshall successfully argued several cases before the Supreme Court, including the 1954 landmark case of *Brown v. Board of Education*, ending racial segregation in public education.

A monument honoring Thurgood Marshall was first conceived in December 1976 by city officials, using $55,000 in federal housing and community development urban renewal funds. A committee was subsequently formed to conduct a nationwide search for a sculptor.

Thurgood Marshall Monument, Pratt Street and Hopkins Place. *Photo by author.*

Forty artists entered the competition, and in May 1977, the committee unanimously selected Baltimore sculptor Reuben Kramer. In September 1977, the city appropriated the necessary funds and signed an agreement with Kramer to create a statue of Marshall and a pedestal.[109]

Dedication of the Thurgood Marshall Monument occurred on May 16, 1980, with about 250 people in attendance. On the podium with Marshall sat five of his fellow Supreme Court justices, Maryland governor Harry Hughes, Mayor William Donald Schaefer and Marshall's longtime friend and associate Clarence M. Mitchell Jr., former director of the NCAAP. During the ceremony, Justice William Brennan called him "one of the great figures of our century." Governor Hughes called him a "symbol of racial progress made in the last half century." In his remarks, Justice Marshall told the audience, "[D]espite the progress made in civil rights, there is much more to be done. I hope that when you see the statue, you won't think this is the end of it. We've got a lot more to do."[110]

The bronze statue, eight feet in height, has a rugged, uneven surface and portrays Marshall in his judicial robes. It rests on a granite pedestal three feet in height that was constructed by the Hilgartner Company of Baltimore.[111]

The inscription on the sidewalk in front of the pedestal reads:

SUPREME COURT JUSTICE
THURGOOD MARSHALL
REUBEN KRAMER, SCULPTOR
19—DEDICATED—80
CITY OF BALTIMORE
WILLIAM DONALD SCHAEFER, MAYOR

WILLIAM DONALD SCHAEFER MEMORIAL

Location: Inner Harbor, Light Street Pavilion
Designer: Rodney Carroll
Erected: 2009

Baltimore mayor, Maryland governor and state comptroller William Donald Schaefer (1921–2011) is honored by this memorial in the form of a sculpture garden near the city's Light Street Pavilion. Created by sculptor Rodney Carroll, the memorial is located on land donated to the city by William

William Donald Schaefer Memorial, Inner Harbor, Light Street Pavilion. *Photo by author.*

Hackerman, chief executive officer of the Whiting-Turner Construction Company and a close friend of Schaefer's.

The larger-than-life statue was unveiled before hundreds of people in Baltimore's Inner Harbor on November 2, 2009, as part of Schaefer's eighty-eighth birthday celebration. The Morgan State University Choir sang, Baltimore City College High School students marched and Baltimore City Police and Fire Department units were present. The event included Maryland politicians, including Maryland governor Martin O'Malley and Mayor Sheila Dixon.

Others in attendance included members of Congress Steny Hoyer and Kweisi Mfume, former Maryland governors Robert Ehrlich and Marvin Mandel and State Comptroller Peter Franchot. Governor O'Malley described Schaefer as "a great citizen, a great neighbor, and a great man to lead us through these important years." The crowd serenaded Schaefer with "Happy Birthday" as confetti shot into the sky and flags surrounding the statue were lifted away.

Schaefer responded by saying, "Thank you for coming. You don't know what it means to me, when you're in the sort of twilight of your life."[112]

The eight-foot bronze likeness of Schaefer rests on a marble base and sits inside a garden setting designed by landscape architect Carol Macht. The statue depicts Schaefer waving his left hand, with his right hand clutching a sheet of paper.

The inscription on the base reads:

WILLIAM DONALD SCHAEFER

Chapter 7

HISTORICAL FIGURES

Simón Bolívar Monument

Location: Bedford Square, North Charles and Saint Paul Streets
Designer: Felix W. DeWeldon
Erected: 1961

As a gesture of friendship and goodwill between the United States and the people of Venezuela, the Venezuelan government presented this bronze bust of the famous South American liberator Simón Bolívar (1783–1830) to the people of Baltimore. The bust is identical to others presented by the Venezuelan government to several American cities. The original work was created in 1958 by Austrian-born sculptor Felix deWelson, who also designed the Marine Corps Iwo Jima Memorial in Arlington, Virginia.

In August 1960, the Venezuelan government offered an exact copy of the Bolívar bust to the City of Baltimore. Mayor J. Harold Grady graciously accepted the gift and asked the board of park commissioners and municipal art commission to find it a suitable location.[113] The two bodies selected Bedford Square, at the confluence of North Charles and Saint Paul Streets, as a location.[114] The Guilford Association, which owned the property, granted the city government easement rights, with title and control of the property remaining with the association.[115]

On April 19, 1961, the 150th anniversary of Venezuelan independence, a crowd of about one hundred persons attended the unveiling of the Simón Bolívar Monument. The exercises commenced with an invocation by Reverend

Simón Bolívar Monument, Bedford Square, North Charles and Saint Paul Streets. *Photo by author.*

John E. Wise of Loyola College. The Second Army Band played the national anthems of the United States and Venezuela. Odell Martin Smith, assistant to Governor J. Millard Tawes, delivered the opening address. The main speaker, Dr. Jose Antonio Mayobre, Venezuelan ambassador to the United States, performed the unveiling. Mayor J. Harold Grady accepted the monument on behalf of the citizens of Baltimore. The ceremony concluded with wreaths being placed at the base of the pedestal by the consuls of Venezuela, Colombia and Ecuador and officers of the Bolivian Society of Baltimore.[116]

The life-size bronze bust of Bolívar surmounts a pedestal of Indiana limestone provided by the city government. The pedestal is five feet in height and bears a small bronze tablet embossed with the national seal of Venezuela.

The inscription on the pedestal reads:

SIMON
BOLIVAR
1783–1830
LIBERATOR
OF
VENEZUELA
COLOMBIA
ECUADOR
PERU
BOLIVIA

CHRISTOPHER COLUMBUS MONUMENT

Location: Harford Road and Parkside Drive
Designer: Unknown
Erected: 1792

This monument in honor of Christopher Columbus (1451–1506) was originally located on the grounds of a country villa about one mile northeast of Baltimore town. In the form of an obelisk, it is believed to be the oldest monument to Columbus in the United States.

In 1783, at the close of the Revolutionary War, several French officers settled in Baltimore. Among them was Charles Francis Adrian le Paulmier Chevakier D'Anmour, the French consul to the United States. In 1789, D'Anmour purchased a tract of land about one mile northeast of town near the present-day intersection of North Avenue and Harford Road. There he built a country villa named Belmont. One evening in 1792, he was entertaining several guests when one of them remarked that America had never erected a monument in honor of its discoverer. D'Anmour set out to correct it immediately by having a monument to Columbus erected on his own estate.

On August 3, 1792, exactly three hundred years after Columbus set sail for the New World, D'Anmour laid the cornerstone. The following account appeared in a national newspaper at the time:

> *Baltimore, August 17th—We are informed by a correspondent, that on Friday, the third of this month, being the anniversary of the departure of Christopher Columbus from Spain, for the voyage in which he discovered the new world; and that day being the third century and secular year of the event that led to the great discovery, the cornerstone of an obelisk, to honor the memory of that immortal man, was laid in a grove, on the gardens of the villa "Belmont," the country seat of the Chevalier D'Anmour, near this town. He adds "that suitable inscriptions are to be fixed to this pedestal on the twelfth of next October, the anniversary of the day on which he, for the first time, saw the land he so eagerly was in quest of."* [117]

France recalled D'Anmour in 1796, and he sold the estate. The property passed through several owners, and the monument fell into obscurity until a federal artillery battery encamped on the estate during the Civil War. Soldiers came upon the hidden obelisk in 1863 while clearing trees and shrubs. After the war, undergrowth once again closed in on the neglected monument.

Christopher Columbus Monument, Harford Road and Parkside Drive. *Photo by author.*

Its existence became known again in 1876 when Johns Hopkins University librarians Arthur Wellington and N. Murray, along with Professor T.C. Murray, stumbled upon it while walking in the country. They found the obelisk of brick and plaster in a cedar tree grove near the remains of the earthworks that had been hastily thrown up during the Civil War.

In 1882, the trustees of the Samuel Ready School for Orphaned Females purchased the property. That same year, historians connected with Johns Hopkins University conducted a careful study of the monument's origin and history. In 1892, Professor Herbert B. Adams concluded that "it is undoubtedly the first monument ever erected in honor of Christopher Columbus in the new world."[118]

In 1937, the Sears Roebuck Company purchased the property, and the monument remained on the company's property for twenty-six years. In 1963, the company offered it to the city, provided the city pay the relocation expenses. The city government accepted the offer, which was approved by the municipal art commission. The city dismantled the monument and reerected it on park property at Harford Road and Parkside Drive.[119]

On Columbus Day, October 12, 1964, a rededication ceremony was held at its new location. The exercises were opened with an invocation by

Reverend Monsignor Thomas Whelan of the Cathedral of Mary Our Queen, followed by the playing of "The Star-Spangled Banner" and "Maryland, My Maryland." Addresses were delivered by park board president Frank Marino; Gilbert Kunz, general manager of the Sears Roebuck Company; and city council president Thomas D'Alesandro III. A wreath was laid at the base by Mayor Theodore McKeldin and Judge Vito Marino, chair of the Columbus Day Commission. The exercises concluded with a benediction by Monsignor Whelan.[120]

The monument consists of a plain pedestal and shaft, constructed of brick said to have been imported from England. Originally covered with plaster, it is now covered with a coating of stucco. The obelisk is quadrangular in form, sloping in diameter from two feet, six inches at its top to six feet, six inches at its base. The pedestal itself is five feet, six inches in diameter and ten feet in height. The monument is ornamented by a capstone approximately eighteen inches in height. The pedestal surmounts a base approximately thirty inches in height. The total height is forty-four feet, seven inches from ground to pinnacle. A marble slab, approximately two feet, six inches by four feet, with a dedicatory inscription, is attached to the western face of the pedestal.

The inscription on the marble slab reads:

SACRED
TO THE
MEMORY
OF
CHRIS.
COLUMBUS
OCTOB. XII
MDCCIIIC

CHRISTOPHER COLUMBUS MONUMENT

Location: Druid Hill Park
Designers: Achille Canessa, Albert Weinert
Erected: 1892

Overlooking the lake in Druid Hill Park stands a statue of Christopher Columbus (1451–1506) by New York sculptor Albert Weinert. Erected by the city's Italian community, the statue is a replica of one created by Italian sculptor Achille Canessa.

In 1892, the Italian Society of Baltimore held a meeting to consider ideas for a fitting quadricentennial celebration of Columbus's arrival in what is now known as the Americas. After much discussion, a suggestion was made to present the city with a statue of Columbus. The proposal met with unanimous approval, and plans were formulated to achieve the goal.

The Columbus Monument subscription fund was established, and within a few weeks, a committee was appointed to obtain designs for the monument.[121] The committee subsequently secured the services of New York sculptor Albert Weinert, who created a statue of Columbus based on the original by Albert Canessa of Genoa, Italy.[122] After considering three locations, the committee selected a grassy knoll in Druid Hill Park, which received the approval of the park board.[123]

Dedication of the Columbus Monument occurred on October 12, 1892, preceded by a parade of Italian American societies from Baltimore and Washington, D.C. James Cardinal Gibbons gave the benediction, followed by the main address from historian and author A. Leo Knott. Additional speeches were made in Italian by Giovanni Schiaffino, Prospero Schiaffino and E.M. Scogamillo and in English by Richard M. McSherry, Reverend J.L. Andreis and the Spanish consul Don Luis Marinas. Mayor Ferdinand Latrobe, representing the citizens of Baltimore, accepted the monument from M. Vacarri.[124]

The monument stands nineteen feet, six inches high and is made entirely of white marble. The pedestal, constructed by L. Hilgartner and Sons of Baltimore, is thirteen feet in height and consists of three steps, a series of moldings, a die-block, a molded cap and a plinth for the statue. The statue, with a height of six feet, six inches, depicts Columbus standing bareheaded against a balustrade of gray, from which hangs a mooring ring. He is holding a half-opened chart in his right hand, while his left hand rests on a globe. A bronze wreath on the pedestal was subsequently added by local Italian American societies.

The inscription on the pedestal reads:

To
Christoforo Colombo
The
Italians
Of Baltimore
1892

Christopher Columbus Monument, Druid Hill Park. *Photo by author.*

FRANCIS SCOTT KEY MONUMENT

Location: Eutaw Place and Lanvale Street
Designer: Jean M.A. Mercie
Erected: 1911

Located in a beautifully landscaped setting on Eutaw Place stands a monument in honor of Francis Scott Key (1779–1843), author of "The Star-Spangled Banner."

In December 1906, only a few weeks before his death, Charles L. Marburg, a wealthy Baltimore businessman, entrusted $25,000 to his brother Theodore for the purpose of erecting a monument in honor of Key.[125] Marburg stipulated that it was to be erected in the city of Baltimore provided that the city government donate and prepare the site. As a location, Marburg suggested the intersection of Eutaw Place and Lanvale Street, which received the unanimous approval of the municipal art commission.[126] The city council approved the project in April 1908.[127]

In April 1907, Theodore Marburg commissioned the distinguished French sculptor Jean Marius Antonin Mercie to design and create the monument.[128] In March 1908, Mercie submitted his design to the municipal art commission, where it received a favorable endorsement.[129]

A crowd of thousands attended the dedication of the Francis Scott Key Monument on May 15, 1911, including several Key descendants. The exercises opened with the Fifth Regiment Field Band playing patriotic music. On the dignitary stand sat members of the Francis Scott Key Chapter, Daughters of the American Revolution; Mayor J. Barry Mahool; James Cardinal Gibbons; and Theodore Marburg.

In a lengthy address, the main speaker, W. Stuart Symington, praised the life and career of Francis Scott Key. Mayor Mahool accepted the monument and expressed the gratitude of the citizens of Baltimore. The ceremony concluded with an unveiling of the monument by Mrs. William Gilmore, a granddaughter of Francis Scott Key, and five-year old Charles Marburg, son of Theodore Marburg.[130]

The monument is a remarkable example of detail. At the foot of the four-pillared central form is a small boat. A bronze likeness of Key is standing at the rear of the boat with outstretched arms, holding the manuscript of "The Star-Spangled Banner" in his left hand. A bronze sailor is shown at the front of the boat, with oars in hand. The boat is surrounded by waves, fashioned from white stone, from which it and the central form is carved.

Francis Scott Key Monument, Eutaw Place and Lanvale Street. *Photo by author.*

Waves join the waters of the basin in which the whole group is set. The gilded figure of Columbia, holding an American flag, surmounts the top of the central form.

A round vessel, originally intended to be a fountain, is found within the four pillars of the central form. The original plans were altered, however, to fill the basin from hidden jets. Bronze tablets situated on the sides are engraved with scenes depicting the attack on Fort McHenry. Just below the figure of Columbia on the cornice of the central form is inscribed the word "KEY."

The inscription on the front of the monument reads:

Francis Scott Key
1779–1843

Presented to the City of Baltimore by
Charles L. Marburg

FRANCIS SCOTT KEY MONUMENT

Location: Fort McHenry National Monument
Designer: Chales H. Niehaus
Erected: 1922

Fort McHenry National Monument serves as an appropriate location for this monument, which honors Francis Scott Key (1779–1843) and the soldiers and sailors who defended Baltimore from the British during the War of 1812. For it was from Fort McHenry, on the morning of September 14, 1814, where the American flag was flying that inspired Key to write "The Star-Spangled Banner."

In 1912, Baltimore held a series of events to commemorate the centennial of the War of 1812. As part of the commemoration, Maryland congressman John C. Linthicum introduced a bill in Congress appropriating $75,000 to "[e]rect at Fort McHenry under the direction of the Secretary of War, a monument in memory of Francis Scott Key and the soldiers and sailors who participated in the Battle of North Point and the attack on Fort McHenry in the War of Eighteen Hundred and Twelve."[131] Congress enacted the legislation and authorized the secretary of war to form a committee for the "purpose of preparing the plans and selecting a site for the monument."[132]

Soon after its establishment, the Francis Scott Key Monument Committee contacted the National Commission of Fine Arts requesting advice as to a location and design. The Commission of Fine Arts, however, suggested that the secretary of war employ an independent architect for such a purpose. Secretary of War Lindley M. Garrison subsequently appointed a three-member committee consisting of architects Joseph E. Sperry and Douglass Thomas Jr. and sculptor Ephraim Keyser to act as advisors in determining a site and preparing a program of competition for selecting a suitable design.

After some deliberation, the advisory committee selected the Fort Avenue entrance to Fort McHenry as a suitable location for the monument.[133] To select a design, the advisory committee appointed a five-member jury composed of architects Glen Brown, Herman McNeil and A.A. Weinman, Congressman John Linthicum and Mayor James Preston. After examining the thirty-four models submitted, and on the recommendation of the jury, Secretary of War Newton D. Baker

Francis Scott Key Monument, Fort McHenry National Monument. *Photo by author.*

awarded the commission to New York sculptor Charles D. Niehaus.[134] In responding to the selection, one popular newspaper reported, "The fact that the work is to be done by Mr. Niehaus will be a magnificent achievement. He is regarded by the foremost critics as the greatest sculptor this country has ever produced."[135]

Niehaus completed work on the sculpture in October 1917. With the entry of the United States into World War I, however, plans for placing the monument at Fort McHenry had to be delayed due to the necessity of converting the fort into a military hospital.[136] As a temporary location, Mayor Preston and city officials sought approval from the War Department to place the sculpture in City Hall Plaza. Secretary of War Baker, after conferring with his legal advisors, denied the request, stating that the temporary location would be contrary to the language in the act authorizing the monument. Furthermore, Secretary Baker cited a National Commission on Fine Arts report that the monument would be proportionally out of scale with the plaza and surrounding buildings.[137]

At the conclusion of the war, plans were once again formulated to place it at Fort McHenry. This time, city officials proposed placing the sculpture about eight hundred feet inside the fort, overlooking the Patapsco River.

The new location received the approval of the Commission of Fine Arts and the secretary of war.[138]

After two years of site preparation, the Francis Scott Key Monument was dedicated on Flag Day, June 14, 1922, with President Warren G. Harding in attendance. The presidential motorcade was greeted at the city line by a reception committee in more than a dozen cars. Following a luncheon at the Emerson Hotel, the presidential party drove through the crowd-lined streets to Fort McHenry.

Upon entering the fort, President Harding stepped from his vehicle and met with patients of the military hospital located on the grounds. The president took his place on the stage as the crowd cheered and General Pershing's own band played "Hail to the Chief." Lieutenant Colonel Clarence O. Sherill, personal representative of Secretary of War John Weeks, chair of the dedication ceremonies, introduced Bishop John Gardner Murray, who delivered the invocation. Katherine Ethel Broening, daughter of the mayor, and Marie Niehaus, daughter of the sculptor, released the flags covering the monument as a high school chorus sang "The Star-Spangled Banner."

Assistant Secretary of War Matthew Wainwright formally presented the monument to the citizens of Baltimore. Colonel Sherill praised and acknowledged the presence of the sculptor, Charles Niehaus. Congressman Linthicum and Mayor Broening followed with short speeches. President Harding, in delivering his address, complimented the city on its patriotism and expressed the gratitude of the nation to Francis Scott Key and the soldiers and sailors honored by the monument. Following the president's remarks, Right Reverend J.P. Holden gave the closing benediction. The ceremony concluded with the playing of taps.[139]

The forty-five-foot bronze statue depicts Orpheus, playing a harp made from a tortoise shell and ram horns. The statue surmounts a pedestal seven feet in height, with a diameter of fifteen feet. The base is round and classic in design, with seats forming an exedra. A marble band adorned with thirteen carved rosettes, representing the original thirteen states in the Union, surrounds the top of the pedestal.

Carved on the pedestal, in low relief, is a profile portrait of Francis Scott Key inscribed with the dates of his birth and death with garlands, shields and flags. To the right of the portrait is a sailor in armor, with sea horses on his chest, followed by dolphins in a shield, a wreath with the raised word *NAVY* and a young man swinging an incense burner, representing the part played by the local churches on receiving news of the victory by the ringing of bells. Other figures represented are a female and a male dancing and blowing trumpets, as well as an author writing with a dog beside him.

The figures are followed by two males and two females singing, each holding a scroll; a youth playing a harp; a female dancing and blowing a horn; another female dancing and playing cymbals; another youth blowing a trumpet; a female spreading the news of victory; two females blowing trumpets; a youth carrying a manuscript of "The Star-Spangled Banner"; a wreath with the raised word *ARMY*; and a female figure in armor representing the army, with an American eagle on her breastplate, with a shield and snakes entwined.

The Baltimore firm of Ruhlman and Wilson constructed the architectural setting of rose-pink Tennessee marble. The New York firm of Peters and Humphries rendered the marble frieze. The sculpture was cast at the Gorham Company Foundry in Providence, Rhode Island.

The inscription on the pedestal reads:

Born Francis Scott Key Died
1780   1843

To Francis Scott Key author of the Star-Spangled
Banner and to the soldiers and sailors who took
part in the Battle of North Point and the defense
of Fort McHenry in the War of 1812

Charles N. Niehaus, Sculptor
1922

Members of the Francis Scott Key Monument Committee
Hon. William F. Broening, Mayor of Baltimore, honorary chairman
J. Cookman Boyd, president of the park board, chairman
Hon. J. Charles Linthicum, Congressman from the 4th Congressional
    District of Maryland
Hon. John Walter Smith
B.B. Bibbons

MARQUIS DE LAFAYETTE MONUMENT

Location: Mount Vernon Place
Designers: Thomas Hastings and Andrew O'Connor
Erected: 1924

This bronze, equestrian statue of the Marquis de Lafayette (1757–1834) was erected by the City of Baltimore as a sign of gratitude for his service and dedication to the United States. Marie, Joseph Paul Yves Roch Gilbert de Motier, Marquis de Lafayette, a French aristocrat and military officer, fought in the American Revolution, commanding American troops in several battles. When the American cause needed help, Lafayette skillfully solicited funds, soldiers and ships from the king of France. He is admired and held in high esteem by both the United States and France.

In May 1917, a delegation of French officials consisting of the former premier of France and current minister of justice Rene Viviani, Marshal Joseph Joffre, Vice Admiral Paul Chocheprat and Marquis de Chambrun, a descendant of Lafayette, arrived in Baltimore. While in the city, they visited the Washington Monument and expressed a desire for a monument in honor of Washington's friend Lafayette. After the visit, a meeting of several prominent citizens was held in the mayor's office, where pledges were given for the erection of an equestrian statue of Lafayette.

To oversee construction, Mayor Preston appointed an executive committee, which established the Lafayette Monument Fund to solicit donations.[140] Contributions arrived from the city schools, individuals, patriotic societies and other public organizations.

In 1918, the executive committee commissioned Thomas Hastings, a well-known architect, and Andrew O'Connor, a world-renowned sculptor, to create the monument.[141] As a location, the two artists selected a plot of ground in Mount Vernon Place close to the Washington Monument on land donated by John Eager Howard, a close friend of George Washington. Howard, himself, had a monument in the square. Therefore, it was thought that the two friends of Washington, Lafayette and Howard, should have their monuments fittingly grouped together in Mount Vernon Place.

A heated controversy developed, however, when news circulated that Mount Vernon Place was selected as the location. Several influential citizens opposed the proposed location, believing that it "would be a serious mistake and mar that beautiful spot."[142] Most of the municipal art commission members opposed the proposed site as well and suggested other locations.

The controversy continued for more than four years until Mayor Howard Jackson decided the issue, confirming that the monument would remain in Mount Vernon Place.[143]

Official dedication of the Lafayette Monument occurred on September 6, 1924, attended by President Calvin Coolidge; the French Charge d' Affaires, Andre de LaBoulaye; Maryland governor Albert Ritchie; Baltimore mayor Howard Jackson; representatives of foreign governments; and other prominent persons. More than twenty thousand persons attended the ceremony, which opened with the "Call to Colors" by the buglers of the Twelfth United States Infantry. An invocation was delivered by Reverend Joseph Cunnane, pastor of St. Andrew's Catholic Church. After the playing of "Baltimore, Our Baltimore" by the assembled bands, addresses were made by Mayor Jackson and former mayor James Preston. Ella Galloway, daughter of Mayor Jackson, and Kathryn Boyd, daughter of park board president J. Cookman Boyd, pulled the ropes to remove the canvas and revealed the equestrian statue of Lafayette as the crowd sang "America."

Following the unveiling, messages were delivered from Premier Herriot and President Deumergue of France by Maurice Leon, chair of the Lafayette

Marquis de Lafayette Monument, Mount Vernon Place. *Photo by author.*

Day National Committee. Andre de LaBoulaye gave a short address followed by the playing of "The Star-Spangled Banner." At this point, President and Mrs. Coolidge descended from the platform and placed a wreath at the base. President Coolidge's speech was the last on the program, and it was followed by the playing of "Maryland, My Maryland." The ceremony concluded with a benediction by Reverend Oscar Olson, pastor of Mount Vernon Episcopal Church. A copper box containing a copy of the president's address, the official program, invitations to the ceremony, an engraved reply of the president and copies of local newspapers were placed in the pedestal.[144]

The sixteen-foot, nine-inch-tall bronze statue depicts Lafayette as a nineteen-year-old major general in the Continental army of the United States. He is seated on a prancing horse facing south. The sculpture rests atop a tall rectangular base with steps surrounding it.

The inscription on the pedestal reads:

[Front]
LA FAYETTE
1757–1834

[West Side]
LAFAYETTE IMMORTAL
BECAUSE A SELF-FORGETTABLE SERVANT OF
JUSTICE AND HUMANITY
BELOVED BY ALL AMERICANS
BECAUSE HE ACKNOWLEDGED NO DUTY MORE
SACRED THAN TO FIGHT FOR THE FREEDOM OF HIS FELLOW MAN
WOODROW WILSON

[East Side]
EN 1777 LAFAYETTE TRAVERSANT LES MERS
AVEC DES VOLONTAIRES FRANCAIS
EST VENUE APPORTER UNE AIDE FRATERNELLE
AU PEOPLE AMERICAIN
QUI COMBATTAIT POUR LIBERTE NATIONALE

IN 1917 LA FRANCE COBATAITTAIT A SON TOUR POUR DEFENDER SAVIE
EST LA LIBERTE DU MONDE L'AMERIQUE QUI N'AVAIT
JAMAIS OUBLIE LAFAYETTE, A TRAVVEISE LES MERS
POUR AIDER LA FRANCE, ET LA MONDE AN ETE SAUVE
R. POINCARE

NATIVE AMERICAN MONUMENT

Location: Clifton Park, Saint Lo and Indian Drives
Designer: Edward Berge
Erected: 1916

This statue of a Native American titled *On the Trail* is a representational sculpture dedicated to America's first inhabitants. It was presented to the citizens of Baltimore by the Peabody Institute, which purchased it through the Rinehart Fund. Established by American sculptor William Henry Rinehart, the fund provided scholarships for gifted young artists at the Maryland Institute College of Art. The statue was designed and created by Edward Berge, himself a Rinehart scholar.

Acting Mayor John Hubert, during a meeting of the municipal art commission, approved and accepted the gift on behalf of the city. Clifton Park was approved as a location by the board of park commissioners.[145]

The formal presentation of the *On the Trail* statue occurred on October 6, 1916, attended by Mayor James H. Preston, members of the municipal

Native American Monument, Clifton Park, St. Lo and Indian Head Drives. *Photo by author.*

art commission and trustees of the Peabody Institute. Upon seeing the statue, Mayor Preston remarked, "I regard the statue as being one of the finest examples of statuary of this period, and perhaps in the country…it is full of action, beautifully modeled, and a very strong presentation of the Indian character."[146]

The bronze statue stands approximately seven feet, four inches in height. The figure is depicted shading his eyes with his left arm while looking across an open field. His attire consists of a loin cloth, moccasins on his feet and a single feather on his head. His bow and arrows are hanging down his back. The statue surmounts a base of rough-hewn Harford County, Maryland flint stone measuring seven feet by five feet.

The inscription on the base reads:

On the Trail

Presented by the Peabody Institute of the city of Baltimore

William H. Rinehart Fund 1916
Edward Berge, Sculptor

WILLIAM WALLACE MONUMENT

Location: Druid Hill Park
Designer: D.W. Stevenson
Erected: 1893

On the west side of the lake in Druid Hill Park stands an imposing bronze statue of the Scottish patriot Sir William Wallace (1270–1305), who led a revolt against King Edward I of England. Wallace spent most of his life battling with English forces for Scottish independence. The story of his life has stirred the national pride of Scots for more than six hundred years and inspired the 1995 film *Braveheart*.

Beginning in 1905, the Saint Andrew's Society has used the Wallace statue as the location for the celebration of Saint Andrew's Day, the anniversary of William Wallace's death.

Successful Baltimore banker William Wallace Spence, a former president of the Saint Andrew's Society of Baltimore and descendant of William Wallace, presented the statue to the city in honor of his personal hero. He

William Wallace Monument, Druid Hill Park. *Photo by author.*

saw the statue while traveling through Scotland and ordered a replica copy at a cost of $20,000. The original was sculpted in 1881 by D.W. Stevenson, a member of the Royal Academy in Scotland.[147]

The William Wallace Monument was dedicated on Saint Andrew's Day, November 30, 1893, with more than twelve thousand people in attendance. The ceremony began with a procession to the site from the park gate on Mount Royal Avenue. William Wallace Spence—along with Mayor Ferdinand Latrobe, members of the city council and the British consul—occupied a stand just a few yards from the monument. Members of Baltimore's Saint Andrew's Society and the Caledonian Club of Washington, in native costumes (kilts and capes), gathered around the monument. A band with Scottish pipers played several selections.

The exercises opened as President John T. Morris of the Saint Andrew's Society gave a welcoming address and thanked William Wallace Spence for the gift; Spence, in turn, delivered an address and formally presented the monument to the city. At this point, the pipers played the tune "Highland Lassie," as Louisa Wallace Hazlehurst, the great-granddaughter of William Wallace Spence, pulled the cord that brought down the covering. Mayor

Latrobe accepted it on behalf of the city with a brief address. The exercises concluded with a benediction by Reverend George Currie, rector of Christ's Protestant Episcopal Church, and the singing of "Auld Lang Syne."[148]

The bronze statue of Wallace, cast in Munich, Germany, is fourteen feet in height. He is standing and holding a sword above his head and clothed in linked chain armor from head to foot over which a light cloak, reaching to his knees, is draped. He is wearing a kilt-like dress. Around his waist are two straps, to one of which is attached a bone horn. He has a helmet on his head. His left hand rests on a shield, which has a large lion depicted. His bearded face has an expression of determination and courage. The figure is mounted atop a pedestal made of rough-hewn granite measuring thirteen feet in height and carved by William H. Johnson of Baltimore.

The inscription on the front of the pedestal reads:

WALLACE
PATRIOT AND MARTYR
FOR
SCOTTISH LIBERTY
1305

The inscription on the bronze tablet on the back of the pedestal reads:

PRESENTED
BY
WILLIAM WALLACE SPENCE
TO THE CITY OF BALTIMORE
1893

GEORGE WASHINGTON MONUMENT

Location: Druid Hill Park
Designer: Edward Sheffield Bartholomew
Erected: 1859; Re-erected: 1892

Of all the notables in the history of the United States, there is no individual more revered than George Washington (1732–1799), who led the American army to victory during the American Revolution and became the first president of the United States.

George Washington Monument, Druid Hill Park. *Photo by author.*

In 1857, Noah Walker, a wealthy Baltimore merchant, was constructing a new building on East Baltimore Street and wrote to his son, Noah Dixon Walker, in Europe, instructing him to purchase a statue of George Washington for the front of the building. Based on the recommendation of Baltimore businessman Enoch Pratt, Noah Dixon Walker commissioned Edward Bartholomew, an American sculptor living in Italy, to create the statue at a cost of $6,000. Walker placed the statue in a niche on the second story of his building, where it was illuminated at night by a circle of gas-lit stars.

Noah Walker died in 1874 and was survived by his son, who died twelve years later. In 1892, the grandchildren of Noah Walker sold the Washington Building but removed the statue as part of the sale. That same year, the family presented it to Mayor Ferdinand Latrobe and the citizens of Baltimore. The donation was made under the condition that the city bear the cost of removing it and locating a pedestal. Furthermore, the Walker family wanted the statue placed somewhere in Druid Hill Park.[149] Without a back, the statue had to be placed in a niche again, which was made by George Mann and Son. The pedestal, a gift from Enoch Pratt, was made by the firm of Nardin and Weber.[150]

The figure of George Washington is full-length. He is depicted with a scroll in his right hand, holding it against his chest. His left hand is resting on a book lying on a small stand at his side. A military cloak surrounds his shoulders. The base is made of rough granite, and the niche is made of polished granite.

The inscription on the front of the pedestal reads:

Presented
By the Family of
Noah Walker

The inscription on the back of the pedestal reads:

Pedestal	Statue
From	From
Enoch Pratt	Noah Walker

GEORGE WASHINGTON MONUMENT

Location: Mount Vernon Place
Designers: Robert Mills (Architect), Henrico Causisi (sculptor)
Erected: 1815

This monument in honor of George Washington (1732–1799) is one of the most visited in the city. It was the first architecturally designed monument to Washington in the nation and serves as the focal point for the historic Mount Vernon neighborhood. When first erected in 1815, it stood on a hill overlooking Baltimore, but it has since been engulfed by an expanded city. Over the years, it has become an established tourist attraction and the location of many civic events.

In 1809, ten years after Washington's death, several leading citizens of Baltimore petitioned the Maryland legislature to authorize a lottery to raise money for the construction of a monument in his honor. One year later, the legislature passed an act establishing a board of managers empowering them to raise $100,000 and to oversee construction. The board of managers, consisting of twenty-four prominent Marylanders from Baltimore and its environs, had complete control over the selection of a design. The legislation further specified that it must be erected on the site of the city's old courthouse on Calvert Street, between Fayette and Lexington Streets, which was being demolished.[151]

During the winter of 1810, the managers contacted the French architect Maximilian Godefroy and requested that he submit designs for the monument. Of the designs submitted by Godefroy, none was accepted. In March 1813, the managers held a competition offering $500 for the "best design, model, or plan for a monument to the memory of General Washington." Entries were to be submitted by the January 1, 1814 deadline and were to include cost estimates not to exceed $100,000. It is unknown how many designs were submitted, but only four entries have survived.

The first of the known entries was submitted by Maximilian Godefroy, who again entered one of the designs he created in 1810. The second entry was submitted by Joseph Ramee, also from France. A third was submitted anonymously. Robert Mills, an architect from Charleston, South Carolina, submitted the fourth entry. The board of managers, after serious consideration, awarded the $500 cash prize to Robert Mills and named him supervisor of construction.

George Washington Monument, Mount Vernon Place. *Photo by author.*

Mills's design was a massive column resting on a vaulted base. At its summit was a statue of Washington dressed as a Roman warrior riding a chariot. The column, including the statue, was to be 140 feet high.[152] Mills made many changes to the design over the years until it came to look much different from the original.

The first three lottery drawings raised $82,000, which was enough money to begin construction.[153] An event occurred in September 1814, however, that changed the managers' plans. The United States had been at war with Great Britain for more than two years when a British invasion of Baltimore was repulsed on September 13–14, 1814. Plans were then developed to erect a monument in honor of those who had fallen in defense of the city. The managers agreed to give up their site in Courthouse Square so the Battle Monument could be erected there. This, however, required (and received) approval from the state legislature.[154] A new location for the Washington Monument was acquired in 1815 when Colonel John Eager Howard donated a parcel of land just north of the city boundary. The site was carved from the southern portion of Howard's estate, Belvedere, located directly in line with Charles Street. That same year, the state legislature approved the new site.[155]

Construction began on the Washington Monument in the spring of 1815. On July 4, 1815, a cornerstone was laid with a formal Masonic ceremony. Washington himself was a Mason. The militia paraded and bands played patriotic music, including "Yankee Doodle." A salute of thirty-nine guns boomed out, one for each year of American independence. Several clergymen offered prayers, and James A. Buchanan, president of the board of managers, delivered an address praising the life of George Washington. Levin Winder, grand master of the Masons, with managers Mayor Edward Johnson, General Samuel Smith and Colonel John Eager Howard, witnessed and laid hands on the stone. A copper plate with all the managers' names inscribed was deposited in the stone, along with a glass bottle that contained a likeness of Washington, a copy of his farewell address, several newspapers and a few United States coins. The exercises concluded with a one-hundred-gun salute. That night, fireworks were hurled into the sky over the city from Howard's estate and from the new American frigate *Java* in the harbor.[156]

Work began shortly after the cornerstone-laying ceremony. Stonecutters Thomas Towson, William Steuart and Sater Stevenson began constructing the base, using marble donated by Charles Ridgely of Hampton, Baltimore County. The base was completed by 1818, and the column rose to a height of forty-two feet. By 1824, the column was complete, as was the pedestal that was to hold the statue.

After nearly ten years of work, expenses had grown significantly. Although the state legislature had limited the cost to $100,000, more than $113,000 had been spent and the monument was far from completion. The lotteries were no longer producing revenue, and the managers were forced to return to the legislature for additional funds. The assistance was provided over the following fifteen years, but the legislature was assured that completion of the work would be done in the most frugal way. Despite pressure from the managers and Robert Mills, only enough money was allocated to complete essential work. This resulted in further simplification of the design.

Originally, Mills wanted his grand column constructed in seven sections, with the bottom six inscribed with each year of the Revolutionary War from 1776 to 1781. At each separation, there was to be iron-grilled balconies. There was also to be a trophy at each of the four corners of the base. To cut down on expenses, the balconies were eliminated, as were all the fancy designs and words that would have covered the column. The trophies were omitted, as was the Roman chariot idea.

In September 1826, the managers advertised for proposals, designs and estimates from sculptors interested in creating a statue of Washington for the top of the monument. There was little response to the notice, with only three designs received. The managers selected the model submitted by Henrico Causici of Verona, Italy. Causici agreed to create the fifteen-ton statue for $9,000, and the price included the cost of the marble and hoisting the statue to the summit.[157]

Causici began his two-year task in the spring of 1827, working on a thirty-seven-ton block of white marble excavated from a York Road quarry. When finished, the work consisted of three large segments, each weighing about five tons. The large figure of Washington holding a scroll in an outstretched hand depicts the historic moment when he resigned his commission as commander-in-chief of the Continental army. As the work neared completion, Causici found himself unable to raise the statue to the summit and subcontracted the work to Robert Mills, who called in Captain James D. Woodside of the Washington Navy Yard. Woodside was a specialist in rigging and devised a system of pulleys, levers and braces to do the job.[158]

The first two segments were raised in the fall of 1829. The third and final segment was raised with a ceremony on November 25, 1829, witnessed by thousands of spectators. The Third Division of the Maryland Militia, under the command of Major General Samuel Smith, formed a square around the monument. Invited guests, city and state officials and the board of managers occupied seats on a platform at the south side. A second platform was occupied by surviving soldiers of the American Revolution. As the machinery began to move, the band played "Washington's March." In about an hour, the statue of Washington was placed on top as the crowd cheered. The ceremony concluded with a salute of thirteen guns.[159]

More than $200,000 was spent constructing the Washington Monument. In 1843, it was given over to the custody of the Baltimore City government. Over the years, thousands of visitors have climbed the circular steps inside the monument to the observation balcony.

Significant dimensions of the Washington Monument (from original records of the architect, Robert Mills, in the possession of the Maryland Historical Society) include the following:

- Area of ground covered by the monument: 3,800 feet
- Square of the grand base: 50 square feet
- Height of the grand base: 25 feet
- Diameter of the column at the base: 20 feet
- Square of the platform on the capital: 19 feet, 6 inches
- Height of the pedestal to the foot of the statue: 20 feet
- Height of the statue: 16 feet, 6 inches
- Weight of the statue: 16 tons
- Total height of the monument: 178 feet

The Washington Monument Board of Managers included the following: James A. Buchanan, George Comegys, Washington Hall, Lemuel Taylor, Robert Gilmore Jr., George Hoffman, Isaac McKim, Edward J. Coale, William H. Winder, James Partridge, David Winchester, Nicholas G. Ridgely, Fielding Lucas Jr., Robert Miller, James Calhoun Jr., Nathaniel F. Williams, James Williams, Benjamin H. Milliken, James Barroll and Eli Simpkins.

The inscription directly over each of the four doors of the base read:

TO
GEORGE WASHINGTON
BY THE
STATE OF MARYLAND

The inscription beside each door reads:

[SOUTH SIDE]
[LEFT DOOR]
BORN
22 FEBRUARY
1732
[RIGHT DOOR]
DIED
14 DECEMBER
1799

[NORTH SIDE]
[LEFT DOOR]
TRENTON
26 DECEMBER
1776
[RIGHT DOOR]
YORKTOWN
19 October
1781

[EAST SIDE]
[LEFT DOOR]
COMMANDER-IN-CHIEF
OF THE
AMERICAN ARMY
15 JUNE
1775
[RIGHT DOOR]
COMMISSION RESIGNED
AT ANNAPOLIS
26 DECEMBER
1783

[WEST SIDE]
[LEFT DOOR]
PRESIDENT
OF THE
UNITED STATES
4 March
1789
[RIGHT DOOR]
RETIRED
TO MOUNT VERNON
4 March
1797

Chapter 8

MILITARY VETERANS

Black War Veterans Memorial

Location: War Memorial Plaza
Designer: James E. Lewis
Erected: 1972

An anonymous donor provided $30,000 for this memorial to commemorate the wartime contributions of members of the United States military of African descent. The bronze statue is the work of Professor James E. Lewis, former chairperson of the Art Department at Morgan State University. Lewis won a nationwide competition in 1968 to create the statue.

A small controversy developed when Lewis notified the board of park commissioners of the gift and his intention to place the statue in Battle Monument Square, at Lexington and Calvert Streets. The board of park commissioners voted to accept it over the objections of member Harry D. Kaufman, who believed that it should have been erected in honor of a particular individual of African American heritage who "because of bravery and valor distinguished himself and was worthy to be commemorated."[160]

In July 1968, the park board approved the north end of Battle Monument Square as a location.[161] The following October, the municipal art commission endorsed the location and gave its approval to the design.[162] The decision ignited another controversy that lasted for two years. Several community groups, including the Society of the War of 1812, objected to the Battle Monument Square location, believing that it would detract from the historical significance of the Battle Monument itself.

Black War Veterans Memorial, War Memorial Plaza. *Photo by author.*

On October 13, 1971, a heated debate occurred during a park board meeting between Professor Lewis and those groups opposed to the memorial and its proposed location.[163] The park board subsequently stayed with its original decision and retained Battle Monument Square as the location. In addition, the commission for historical and architectural preservation unanimously adopted a resolution supporting the decision.[164]

Dedication of the Black War Veterans Memorial occurred on June 12, 1972, with a brief ceremony. Former Maryland governor Theodore R. McKeldin presided over the exercises and delivered the main address.[165]

In 2007, the African American Patriots Consortium, in a unanimous vote, requested that the memorial be relocated to the renovated War Memorial Plaza across from city hall. The city government granted the request, and it was moved it to its present location on January 12, 2007.

The bronze statue of a Black soldier, weighing 1,500 pounds and standing thirteen feet in height, rests on a marble pedestal five feet in height. The figure is depicted in a modern battle dress uniform and holding a wreath emblazoned with the dates of the major wars of the United States.

The inscription on the bronze tablet attached to the pedestal reads:

DEDICATED TO THE
MEMORY OF
THE NEGRO HEROES
OF THE UNITED STATES
"SLEEP IN PEACE
SLAIN IN THY COUNTRY'S WARS"
A GIFT TO
THE CITY OF BALTIMORE
BY AN ANONYMOUS DONOR
SCULPTOR, JAMES E. LEWIS

GRAND ARMY OF THE REPUBLIC VETERANS MEMORIAL

Location: Federal Hill Park
Designer: Conrad M. Seubott
Erected: 1933

Just inside the Warren Avenue entrance to Federal Hill Park stands a sundial erected as a memorial to those veterans who served in the Union army during the Civil War, 1861–65. Created by Baltimore stonemason Conrad M. Seubott, it was presented to the City of Baltimore by Mother Sperling Tent Number 1, Daughters of the Union Veterans of the Civil War.[166]

The dedication ceremony occurred on April 23, 1933. George T. Leech, commander of the Maryland Department, Grand Army of the Republic, delivered the main address. Remarks were also made by Mayor Howard Jackson, former mayor William Broening and John R. King, a former commander-in-chief of the Veterans of Foreign Wars. Reverend Murray Wagner pronounced the benediction. Mollie Cross, former president of the Daughters of Union Veterans of the Civil War, made the official presentation.[167]

The inscription on the sundial reads:

THE KISS OF THE SUN FOR PARDON
THE SONG OF THE BIRDS FOR MIRTH
ONE IN NEARER GOD'S HEART IN A GARDEN
THEN ANYWHERE ELSE ON EARTH
COME ALONG WITH ME
THE BEST IS YET TO BE

Grand Army of the Republic Memorial, Federal Hill Park. *Photo by author.*

The inscription on the front of the pedestal reads:

IN MEMORY OF
THE GRAND ARMY
OF THE REPUBLIC
BY THE DAUGHTERS
OF THE UNION
VETERANS OF THE
CIVIL WAR
1861–1865
MOTHER SPERLING TENT NO. 1
April 23, 1933

MARYLAND ARMY NATIONAL GUARD, TWENTY-NINTH INFANTRY DIVISION MEMORIAL

Location: Dolphin and 29th Division Streets
Designer: unknown
Erected: 1984

In front of Baltimore's Fifth Regiment Armory Building stands a memorial that pays tribute to the Maryland Army National Guard units that were part of the Twenty-Ninth Infantry Division during World War II. Known as the "Blue and Gray Division"—comprising units from Maryland, Virginia, Pennsylvania and the District of Columbia—the division took part in the fighting on Omaha Beach in Normandy, France, on June 6, 1944, D-Day.

On June 6, 1983, the adjutant general of Maryland, Warren D. Hodges, put forth the idea of commemorating the fortieth anniversary of D-Day in 1984. A proposal was subsequently suggested to erect a memorial in the triangular plaza in front of the Fifth Regiment Armory Building to honor the units and men of the Twenty-Ninth Infantry Division, particularly those from Maryland. The project was given to the Maryland National Guard Military Historical Society. Since the land belonged to the City of Baltimore, Mayor William Donald Schaefer granted the society's request to use the site, and the municipal art commission unanimously approved the project.[168]

The Maryland Army National Guard, Twenty-Ninth Infantry Division Memorial, was dedicated on June 10, 1984, with several D-Day veterans in attendance. The program started with a concert by the Two Hundred Twenty-Ninth Army Band, followed by a posting of the colors by the Maryland National Guard Color Guard. The national anthem was sung by Martin Willen, a World War II army veteran, followed by an invocation from Rabbi Manuel M. Poliakoff, chaplain of the Twenty-Ninth Infantry Division. Retired Colonel Bernard Feingold, vice-chairman of the D-Day Memorial Committee, presided over the ceremonies.

The first speaker was Major General John P. Cooper Jr., chair of the D-Day Memorial Committee. He was followed by Brigadier General James P. Fretterd, assistant adjutant general of the Maryland Army National Guard. Ambassador Philip H. Alston, a naval commander during the D-Day invasion, spoke next, followed by Maryland governor Harry Hughes. The memorial was unveiled by D-Day veteran Captain Leroy R. Weddle, from Hagerstown, Maryland. Brigadier General Edmund G. Beacham

Maryland Army National Guard, 29th Infantry Division Memorial, Dolphin and 29th Division Streets. *Photo by author.*

(Ret.), president of the Maryland National Guard Historical Society, made the dedication. Reverend James E. Moore, chaplain of the One Hundred Seventy-Fifth Infantry Regiment, gave a benediction. The exercises concluded with the singing of "America, the Beautiful" by Martin Willen.[169]

The inscription on the front of the memorial reads:

"29 LET'S GO"!
MARYLAND HONORS
THE CELEBRATED WORLD WAR II
29TH INFANTRY "BLUE AND GRAY"
DIVISION U.S. ARMY
INCLUDING UNITS FROM MARYLAND AND
SOLDIERS REPRESENTATIVE OF THE WHOLE
NATION FOR ITS TIDE-TURNING PERFORMANCE
IN THE MOST VITAL DAY AND BATTLE OF THE WAR
"D DAY" JUNE 6, 1944

EMBARKING FROM ENGLAND WHERE IT HAD
TRAINED SINCE OCTOBER 1942, IT ASSAULTED
GERMANY'S "FESTUNG EUROPA" ON OMAHA BEACH
NORMANY, FRANCE, FOLLOWED BY ELEVEN
MONTHS OF CAMPAIGNS, BATTLES, AND
SORTIES IN EUROPE.
NORMANDY
OMAHA BEACH, ISIGNY, ST. LO PERCY, VIRE
NORTHERN FRANCE
BRITANY, BREST, RECOUVRANCE, LECONQUET
RHINELAND
SIEGFRIED LINE, JULICH, MUNCHE-GEADBCH
CENTRAL EUROPE
RUHR VALLEY, DANNENBERG, ELBE RIVER

MARYLAND PARTICULARLY HONORS HER OWN SONS OF THE MARYLAND
NATIONAL GUARD UNITS, NAMED BELOW AS OF "D DAY" THEY TOGETHER
WITH UNITS FROM VIRGINIA, PENNSYLVANIA, AND THE DISTRICT OF
COLUMBIA COMPOSED THE INITIAL VOLUNTEER "BLUE AND GRAY"
DIVISION MOBILIZED FEB. 3, 1941; INACTIVATED JAN. 17, 1946.
HEADQUARTERS 29TH INFANTRY DIVISION AND
SPECIAL TROOP UNITS AS ALLOTTED (BALTIMORE)
115TH INFANTRY (1ST MD.) REGIMENT
(MARYLAND COUNTIES)
175TH INFANTRY (5TH MD.) REGIMENT
(BALTIMORE)
110TH FIELD ARTILLERY BATTALION
(PIKESVILLE) AT THE START AND AFTER WWII
2ND BN. 110TH F.A. REG'T.
104TH MEDICAL BATTALION
(BALTIMORE) FORMER 104TH MED. REG'T.

The inscription on the back of the memorial reads:

REFLECTIONS

"OMAHA BEACH, HOWEVER, WAS A NIGHTMARE, EVEN
NOW IT BRINGS PAIN TO RECALL WHAT HAPPENED THERE

On June 6, 1944. I Have Returned Many Times to Honor The Valiant Men Who Died on that Beach. They Should Never Be Forgotten. Nor Should Those Who Lived to Carry the Day by the Slimmest of Margins. Every Man Who Set Foot on Omaha Beach that Day Was a Hero."

By Nightfall the Situation Had Swung in Our Favor. Personal Heroism and the U.S. Navy Had Carried The Day. We Had by then Landed Close to 35,000 Men And Held a Sliver of Corpse-Littered Beach Five Miles Long and About 1½ Miles Deep. To Wrest that Sliver From the Enemy Cost Us Possibly 2,500 Casualties."

From a General's Life by
Omar N. Bradley, General
Cmdg, U.S. Troops, "D Day"

"Our Country…Will Never Forget the Heroism Of Those Soldiers on Omaha Beach on June 6, 1944. That Was the Faithful Day of the War. On the Fortunes Of that Landing on the Normandy Coast Hung Success or Failure in the War Against Germany. The Troops Met the Test. The Landing Was Made Good, the Beach Taken, the Cliff Stormed, The Fame of the 29th Infantry Division…Handed Down to History. Their Record in the St. Lo Drive In the Breakthrough France, and in the Heavy Fighting that Fall and Winter Gave Further Proof Of Their Soldiering Valor. They Could Always Be Counted On."

Robert P. Patterson
WWI Volunteer, Infantry Major
D.S.C. & Silver Star, 1918, France
Federal Dist. & Circuit Judge, N.Y.
Asst. Sec'y of War, 1940–41
Deputy Sec'y of War 1941–45
Sec'y of War 1945–47

"REMEMBER THE 29TH DIVISION AND THE SPLENDID CONTRIBUTION
IT HAS MADE TO THE PRESENT VICTORY. YOU MEN…BE
PROUD, FLAUNT YOUR…BLUE AND GRAY—THE INSIGNIA WHICH BY
YOUR OWN DEEDS HAS BECOME A NEW SYMBOL OF COURAGE
IN WAR."

CHARLES H. GERHARDT, MAJOR GENERAL
COMMANDING, 29TH INFANTRY DIVISION
AFTER VICTORY IN EUROPE, MAY 1945

The inscription on the back of the base reads:

ERECTED BY THE MARYLAND NATIONAL GUARD MILITARY HISTORICAL
SOCIETY IN COOPERATION WITH THE STATE OF MARYLAND, THE CITY
OF BALTIMORE, AND THE GENEROUS DONORS. DEDICATED JUNE 10, 1984.
IN MEMORY OF "D DAY" 40 YEARS AGO, JUNE 6, 1944, AND THE 29TH
INFANTRY DIVISION OF WORLD WAR II

MARYLAND KOREAN WAR VETERANS MEMORIAL

Location: Canton Waterfront Park
Designer: William F. Kirwin
Erected: 1990

The State of Maryland erected this memorial in honor of its native sons
and daughters who served in the Korean War between 1950 and 1953, often
referred to as "the forgotten war." More than 45,000 Americans died in the
conflict, including 525 Marylanders. The memorial is located on a one-acre,
tree-studded tract that slopes down to the water's edge in Canton Waterfront
Park, on the northwest branch of the Patapsco River.

In July 1986, Governor Harry Hughes established the Korean War Veterans
Memorial Commission at the request of the Maryland General Assembly.
The commission was charged with the responsibility of "[d]eveloping
recommendations for submission to the governor and general assembly as
to the design, construction, and placement of an appropriate memorial."
Furthermore, the memorial should "contain the names of the 525 Maryland
citizens who died for their country during the Korean War along with the
names of those Marylanders still listed as missing in action in that conflict."[170]

The Korean War Veterans Memorial Commission held its first meeting on August 5, 1986. The following October, it approved a plan to conduct public hearings around the state to accept testimony from individuals and organizations regarding the type of memorial as well as site locations. On August 27, 1987, it held a lengthy discussion regarding recommendations for sites. The Canton Waterfront Park in Baltimore City was unanimously approved as the location.

On September 25, 1987, the commission sponsored a planning session in Baltimore's War Memorial Building to determine the memorial's design. Chris Delaporte, director of the city park board, organized the effort and formed a design team consisting of architects Heather Cass and Patrick Pinnell; landscape architects Douglass Allen, Thomas Kramer and Jeanette Anders; lighting expert Luke Tigue; art consultant Randy Gould; and University of Baltimore historian Daniel R. Beirne.

The commission put forth four guidelines for the design team to consider. The memorial should: 1) contain the names of the 525 Marylanders known to have been killed in the Korean War or still missing in action,

Maryland Korean War Veterans Memorial, Canton Waterfront Park. *Photo by author.*

2) be identified or easily identifiable to the public and invite use during the day and evening hours, 3) be in a space that is distinctive within the Canton Waterfront Park and 4) be accessible to a ceremonial area and the harbor walk extension. Using these basic tenets, the design team developed a concept that was approved by both the municipal art commission and the board of park commissioners.[171]

In 1988, the Maryland General Assembly enacted a $750,000 bond bill to fund construction. On June 15, 1989, the Design Advisory Panel of Baltimore City approved the design, thereby completing the approval process for the project. The Maryland Board of Public Works awarded the construction contract to Joseph Aversa and Sons of Baltimore.

Dedication of the Korean War Veterans Memorial took place on May 27, 1990, attended by more than two thousand people. The ceremony drew many elected officials, including the principal speaker, Governor William Donald Schaefer, who said that the reason for the memorial "could be summed up in four words, so we won't forget. It reminds us of the hurt we felt, and the tears shed by family and friends of those who didn't return."[172]

Former U.S. senator Daniel Brewster presided over the ceremony, which included a posting of the colors by the Maryland Army National Guard and a flyover by the One Hundred Seventy-Fifth Tactical Fighter Group. Three chaplains—Captain William Metzdorf (Catholic), Major Paul Grant (Protestant) and Captain Earl Blackman (Jewish)—made remarks.

As part of the ceremony, cannons fired a twenty-one-gun salute, and the Two Hundred Twenty-Ninth United States Army Band played musical selections, including taps. The U.S. flag was raised at half-staff over the memorial. The ceremony concluded with the retiring of the colors by the color guard.[173]

The Korean War Veterans Memorial consists of a two-foot, six-inch-high granite semicircle, the broken circle symbolizing the incomplete war of police action that ended with a truce agreement. Engraved on the northern part of the circle are the names of the Marylanders killed in the conflict. The southern section of the circle has panels containing a history of the war. There is a stone map of the Korean Peninsula embedded in the pavement and running through a rose-colored line, representing the infamous 38th parallel.

Maryland Revolutionary War Patriots Memorial

Location: Mount Royal Avenue and Cathedral Street
Designers: A.L. van der Bergen and William Boyd, sculptors; Hodges and
Leach, architects
Erected: 1901

Maryland played an active role in the Revolutionary War, and this memorial is dedicated to those patriots from Maryland who served in the Continental army. Led by many dedicated officers, the Maryland regiments, or Maryland Line, served with distinction and participated in every battle of the war.

In 1892, the Maryland Society of the Sons of the American Revolution raised $75,000 for the erection of a memorial in the city of Baltimore to "the sons of Maryland, whose patriotism and dauntless courage contributed so largely to the results of that great struggle."[174] Money was raised by individuals and fundraising events such as exhibitions, art displays and dinners. A considerable sum was donated by the Ancient and Honorable Artillery Company of Boston, Massachusetts. That same year, the organization persuaded the city government to contribute $5,000 toward the effort and donate the land.[175] The Maryland House of Delegates and the Maryland State Senate unanimously approved a bill appropriating an additional $5,000 toward the memorial fund.[176]

Sculptor A.L. van der Bergen was commissioned to create the statue, and sculptor William Boyd was commissioned to create the column. Maryland architects Hodges and Leach designed the setting, which received approval from the municipal art commission.[177]

Dedication of the Maryland Revolutionary War Patriots Memorial occurred on October 19, 1901, preceded by a large parade led by members of the Maryland Society, Sons of the American Revolution. They were followed by mounted police officers and soldiers of the Maryland Army National Guard playing martial music. Minutemen from Washington, D.C., appeared next in their Continental army uniforms.

Reverend Dr. Henry Branch, chaplain of the Sons of the American Revolution, started the ceremony with an invocation, followed by a short address from Alfred, historian of the society. The memorial was presented to the society by Colonel William Ridgely Griffith, chair of the memorial committee. Edwin Warfield, president of the society, accepted and, in turn, presented it to Acting Mayor Henry Williams.

Maryland Revolutionary
War Patriots Memorial,
Mount Royal Avenue
and Cathedral Street.
Photo by author.

At this point, speeches were made by Mrs. Donald McLean, regent of the New York chapter, Daughters of the American Revolution, and Walter Seth Logan, president of the General National Society, Sons of the American Revolution. The patriotic songs of "Maryland, My Maryland," "America" and "The Star-Spangled Banner" were sung by the crowd. Following this, the canvas was pulled away, revealing the dedicatory tablets. Three wreaths were then placed at the base by members representing the various chapters of the Daughters of the American Revolution.[178]

The memorial consists of a column on a platform of three steps and topped by a bronze statue of Liberty. The entire memorial—column, base and cap—were cut from a single stone of Maryland granite. Bronze dedicatory tablets are located on the pedestal between the steps and the column. The total height is sixty feet. Liberty is shown holding the Declaration of Independence and a laurel wreath. The bronze tablets contain the coat of arms of the Society of the Sons of the American Revolution, the coat of arms used by Maryland during the American Revolution, the coat of arms of the United States and a thirteen-star American flag. The first tablet lists the events in which Marylanders participated that led to American independence. The second and third tablets list those battles of the American Revolution in which the Maryland Line participated. The fourth tablet states the reason for erecting the memorial.

The inscription on the bronze tablet on the north side of the memorial reads:

The Maryland House Of Assembly
December 20, 1769
"Peggy Stewart" Day October 19, 1774
The Maryland Convention December 8, 1774
Association of Freemen of Maryland
The Conventions of Maryland
The Committee of Safety
The Committee of Observation and Finance
The Committee of Correspondence
Maryland Members of the Continental Congress
Maryland Signers of the Declaration of Independence
Adoption of the Confederate States

The inscription on the bronze tablet on the west side of the memorial reads:

Maryland Riflemen	August 9, 1775
Long Island	August 22–29, 1776
Rear Guard of the Retreat from New York	September 15, 1776
Heights of Harlaem	September 16, 1776
White Plains	October 28, 1776
Maryland Rifles Before Fort Washington	November 16, 1776
Trenton	December 26, 1776
Princeton	January 3, 1777
Staten Island	August 21, 1777
Brandywine	September 11, 1777
Paoli	September 20, 1777
Germantown	October 4, 1777
Defense of Fort Mifflin	October 23, 1777

The inscription on the bronze tablet on the south side of the memorial reads:

Monmouth	June 28, 1778
Stoney Point	June 1, 1779
Scotch Plains	August 25, 1779
Savannah	October 19, 1779

CAMDEN	August 16, 1780
COWPENS	January 17, 1781
REAR GUARD IN RETREAT BEFORE CORNWALLIS	February 10, 1781
GUILFORD COURT HOUSE	March 5, 1781
AUGUSTA	April 16, 1781
HOBKIRKS HILL	April 25, 1781
NINETY-SIX	May 22, 1781
EUTAW SPRINGS	September 8, 1781
YORKTOWN	October 19, 1781

The inscription on the bronze tablet on the east side of the memorial reads:

TO ALL PATRIOTS OF MARYLAND WHO DURING THE
REVOLUTIONARY WAR ON LAND AND SEA IN
GAINING THE INDEPENDENCE OF THE STATE AND OF THESE
UNITED STATES AND TO THE MARYLAND LINE "THE
BAYONETS OF THE CONTINENTAL ARMY"
ERECTED BY
THE MARYLAND SOCIETY OF
THE SONS OF THE AMERICAN REVOLUTION
AND DEDICATED ON OCTOBER 19, 1901
"PEGGY STEWART DAY"

MARYLAND SPANISH-AMERICAN WAR VETERANS MEMORIAL

Location: Fayette Street and Lakewood Avenue
Designers: George Jones, Theo Alice Ruggles Kitson
Erected: 1943

This replica statue by Theo Alice Ruggles Kitson entitled *The Hiker* pays tribute to those Marylanders who served in the Spanish-American War in 1898. Kitson was one of the most prolific and successful American women sculptors of the late nineteenth and early twentieth centuries. When she created this statue in 1906, it became a famous icon of that war and was widely reproduced throughout the United States. Between 1906 and 1965, forty-eight replicas of *The Hiker* were cast by the Gorham Company of

Maryland Spanish-American War Veteran Memorial, Fayette Street and Lakewood Avenue. *Photo by author.*

Providence, Rhode Island, and erected in cities and towns around the country.

Baltimore's memorial to the Spanish-American War veterans was erected in two stages. A concrete cannon mount, designed in 1906 by George Jones, superintendent of public buildings, served as the city's original memorial. On top of it rests a small Spanish mortar, captured in Cuba on August 22, 1898, by sailors on the USS *Dixie*. Many of the sailors were from Baltimore. On March 29, 1906, five officers from the ship formally presented the captured mortar to Mayor E. Clay Timanus.[179] In 1925, it was placed in the newly completed War Memorial Building with a short dedication ceremony.[180]

In 1942, the United Spanish American War Veterans appealed to and received an appropriation of $4,000 from Maryland governor Herbert R. O'Conor to erect a memorial in honor of Maryland veterans of the Spanish-American War.[181] As a fitting memorial, they selected a replica of Kitson's statue.

The Spanish-American War Veterans Memorial was dedicated on June 11, 1943, on a small plot of land selected by the municipal art commission at the intersection of Fayette Street and Lakewood Avenue.[182] William M. Miller, department commander of the United Spanish American War Veterans, presided over the ceremony. Schoolchildren sang patriotic songs, followed by an invocation from Reverend John S. Martin, pastor of St. Vincent's Catholic Church.[183]

In June 1946, the Spanish mortar was transferred from the War Memorial Building to its present location in front of the *Hiker* statue.[184] Today, both the statue and the Spanish mortar serve as a testimonial to those Marylanders who served in the Spanish-American War.

Standing on a marble pedestal approximately six feet in height is the eight-foot, five-inch bronze statue depicting a typical American soldier of 1898. He is dressed for tropical warfare and wears a broad-brimmed hat and open-necked pull-over shirt with sleeves rolled above his elbows. He holds a rifle in both hands at arm's length across his thighs. A half-filled cartridge belt, leggings, a canteen and haversack complete the outfit. He is shown with widely spaced feet and seems prepared for action. His finger is on the trigger, and his left hand clutches the gun barrel.

The inscription on the front of the pedestal reads:

> DEDICATED
> TO THE
> SPANISH WAR VETERANS
> 1898–1902
>
> ERECTED 1943
> PRESENTED BY THE STATE OF MARYLAND
> WILLIAM M. MILLER
> DEPT. COMDR.

The inscription on a bronze tablet of the mortar reads:

> PRESENTED BY
> THE UNITED SPANISH
> WAR VETERANS
> 1925

The inscription around the barrel of the mortar reads:

> CAPTURED BY THE U.S.S. DIXIE
> MANNED BY THE FIRST NAVAL BATTALION, M.N.G.
> FORT CIAMANERA, GUANTANAMO BAY, CUBA, AUG. 22, 1898
> PRESENTED TO MAYOR E. CLAY TIMANUS

MARYLAND UNION SOLDIERS AND SAILORS MONUMENT

Location: Wyman Park, North Charles and 29th Streets
Designers: Adolph A. Weinman, Albert Randolph Ross
Erected: 1909

The State of Maryland erected this monument in honor of its native sons who served in the Union army and navy during the Civil War (1861–65). It was the result of a speech made in 1903 by gubernatorial candidate Edwin Warfield. In his speech, Warfield expressed his hope that a monument would be erected in Baltimore as a tribute to the military veterans who fought to preserve the Union.

After he became governor in 1904, Warfield led an effort to secure funds from the General Assembly for such a monument. During the 1906 legislative session, $25,000 was appropriated for it, under the direction of an eight-member commission composed of Civil War veterans.[185]

The commission sent notices to many sculptors, inviting them to submit designs. More than eighteen of them responded. Every model submitted was anonymous. The commission requested disinterested sculptors and architects to assist in selecting a winning design. The design by New York sculptor Adolph Weinman was the unanimous choice of the commission.[186]

After adjournment of the legislature in 1906, it was discovered that no funds had provided for the foundation. The commission subsequently appealed to and received an appropriation of $1,990 from the city government for the pedestal.[187] As a location, the Mount Royal Terrace entrance to Druid Hill Park was unanimously approved by the park board.[188] The municipal art commission followed by approving the location, as well as the design.[189]

Maryland's Union Soldiers and Sailors Monument was dedicated on November 6, 1909, in the presence of more than fifty thousand people. Members of the regular army and navy, the Maryland National Guard, the Grand Army of the Republic and some five hundred surviving veterans of the Union army participated. Seated on the reviewing stand were Governor Austin Crothers, Mayor J. Barry Mahool and General Hohn R. King, past chair of the Grand Army of the Republic and chair of the monument commission.

The ceremony opened with an invocation by Reverend J. Wynne Jones, pastor of Abbott Memorial Presbyterian Church and past chaplain of the Department of Maryland, Grand Army of the Republic. General King delivered a short speech and formally presented the monument to the

Maryland Union Soldiers and Sailors Monument, Wayman Park, North Charles and 29th Streets. *Photo by author.*

State of Maryland and the City of Baltimore. Both Governor Crothers and Mayor Mahool gave speeches of acceptance. Cords were then pulled releasing the flags covering the monument. Accompanying the unveiling, a salute of twenty-one guns was fired by Battery E of the Third Field Artillery while the band played "The Star-Spangled Banner." Major John Yellott, a veteran from Baltimore County, delivered a speech thanking the people of Maryland for the monument. The sculptor, Albert Weinman, was introduced by General King, followed by a rendition of "Maryland, My Maryland" by the St. Mary's Industrial School Band. The ceremony concluded with a benediction by Reverend B.F. Clarkson.[190]

The monument is composed of a group setting of bronze figures atop a large granite pedestal. Halfway around is a floor of granite with a continuous granite bench. The complete setting includes an exedra, platform of three steps, six stone cannon posts around the pavement, terminals of double wreaths in relief and bronze dedicatory tablets.

The exedra features a Latin inscription. The bronze grouping depicts a soldier turning from plow and anvil to buckle on a sword, attended by

Victory and Bellona. The sides of the pedestal are marked with reliefs in bronze. One portrays a cavalry and infantry charge and the other a naval attack. The back shows military symbols, such as an eagle, a shield, a sword and an anchor.

The inscription on the front of the pedestal reads:

ERECTED BY THE STATE OF
MARYLAND TO COMMEMORATE
THE PATRIOTISM AND HEROIC
COURAGE OF HER SONS WHO
ON LAND AND SEA FOUGHT
FOR THE PRESERVATION
OF THE FEDERAL UNION IN
THE CIVIL WAR
1861–1865

The inscription on the granite bench reads:

SCUTO BONAE VOLUNTATIS CORANASTI NOS
Translated: Thou has crowned us with the protection of thy good will

The inscription on a bronze tablet to the right reads:

Commission—John R. King, Pres.
C. Augustus E. Spencer, Sec.
Richard N. Bowerton
James Campbell Henry F. Dorton
William Stahl Yates Stirling
George W.F. Vernon

The inscription on a bronze tablet to the left reads:

The erection of this monument was authorized by
the General Assembly of Maryland
Act approved April 5, 1906, Chap. 539

Dedicated Nov. 6, 1909

Maryland Vietnam Veterans Memorial

Location: Middle Branch Park, Hanover Street and Waterview Avenue
Designer: Robert Tennenbaum and Michael Elliott
Erected: 1989

On a grassy knoll overlooking Baltimore's Patapsco River stands a memorial inscribed with the names of the 1,046 Maryland men who died in the Vietnam War and the 38 who are still missing. The Vietnam War, which lasted from 1959 until 1975, was the second-longest war in United States history, surpassed only by the war in Afghanistan.

During the 1983 session of the Maryland General Assembly, Delegate Kenneth Masters of Baltimore County introduced a resolution requesting that the governor establish a Vietnam Veterans Memorial Commission. The resolution passed unanimously in the House of Delegates and was sent to the State Senate, where it also passed by a unanimous vote.[191]

Governor Harry Hughes appointed a fifteen-member Vietnam Veterans Memorial Commission, which held its first meeting on June 15, 1984. Fred L. Wineland, a former Maryland secretary of state and Vietnam War veteran, was chosen as chairperson. The commission was authorized to raise the necessary funds, select a location and oversee construction.

The State of Maryland paid $2 million toward the $3 million cost.[192] The final $1 million was paid through various fundraising activities. Contributions came from small businesses, corporations, local governments, veteran organizations, individuals, foundations and special events. One event that raised sizeable donations, The Last Patrol, was a 365-mile, fourteen-day walk across Maryland by Vietnam veterans that began in Oakland on August 9, 1986, and ended in Berlin on August 23, 1986.

In early 1986, the Vietnam Veterans Memorial Commission held a competition, open to all Marylanders, to select a design for the memorial. More than five hundred entries were received by the February 21, 1986 deadline.[193] Eight finalists were chosen by a panel of artists, architects and sculptors from around the country. Architects Robert Tennenbaum and Michael Elliott of Baltimore's quasi-public Market Center Development Corporation submitted the winning entry and received a $15,000 award.[194]

As a location, the commission selected the north slope of historic Federal Hill. A brief groundbreaking ceremony was held at the location on Veterans Day, November 11, 1986, with Maryland governor Harry Hughes and Baltimore mayor William Donald Schaefer in attendance.[195] The Federal

Maryland Vietnam Veterans Memorial, Middle Branch Park, Hanover Street and Waterview Avenue. *Photo by author.*

Hill location, however, met with opposition from the residents of the surrounding neighborhood, claiming that the slope was unstable and subject to a sliding movement. In addition, they claimed that the memorial would decrease the historic value of Federal Hill.

After a study was completed to estimate the cost of stabilizing the slope, along with many heated debates over the issue, the Vietnam Veterans Memorial Commission rejected the Federal Hill location. The location was changed to the current location on Hanover Street.

The Maryland Vietnam Veterans Memorial was dedicated on May 28, 1989, with more than seven thousand people in attendance. On a bunting-draped stage sat former governor Harry Hughes, Governor William Donald Schaefer, Mayor Kurt Schmoke, members of Congress and members of the Maryland Vietnam Veterans Commission.

The dedication activities began with a parade from Reedbird Avenue to Hanover Street to Waterview Avenue. Musical selections were played by the Two Hundred Twenty-Ninth Maryland Army National Guard Band. Catholic Bishop John Ricard delivered the invocation. The official welcome was given by Fred Wineland, chairperson of the Maryland Vietnam Veterans Memorial Commission. Addresses were delivered by former governor Harry Hughes, Mayor William Donald Schaefer and Mayor Kurt Schmoke. The ceremony ended with a flyover by A-10 fighter planes and helicopters from the Maryland Air National Guard.[196]

Constructed by the Baltimore firm of Roy Kirby and Sons, the memorial consists of a gray granite ring, one hundred feet in diameter, bordered by two grassy areas with hedges and blue spruce trees. A five-foot-tall hedge surrounding the ring was designed as a wreath around the 1,046 names and as a shield from the traffic noises. Lighting includes sixteen spires casting narrow lines around the ring symbolizing sixteen years of official United States involvement in Vietnam.

In the center of the memorial stands a long granite block with the following inscription:

MARYLAND VIETNAM VETERANS MEMORIAL

There is a large pole to the right of the block holding the Maryland state flag. To the right of the flag stands another granite block with the date 1959 inscribed. To the right of this block stands another granite block with the following inscription:

THIS MEMORIAL HONORS THE MEN AND WOMEN OF THE STATE OF
MARYLAND WHO SERVED IN THE ARMED FORCES OF OUR NATION
IN THE VIETNAM WAR, WITH SPECIAL TRIBUTE TO THOSE WHO
LOST THEIR LIVES OR WHO REMAIN MISSING IN ACTION.
THEIR NAMES ARE JOINED IN THIS PLACE IN EVERLASTING
REMEMBRANCE

To the right of this block stands sixty-four granite blocks in circular formation inscribed with an alphabetical listing of the 1,046 Marylanders killed or missing in action during the Vietnam War. At the end of the sixty-four blocks stands another granite block with the following inscription:

MARYLANDERS, WHILE IN THIS PLACE, PAUSE TO RECALL OUR
NATION'S IDEALS, ITS PROMISE, ITS ABUNDANCE, AND OUR
CONTINUING RESPONSIBILITIES TOWARD THE SHARED
FULFILLMENT OF OUR ASPIRATIONS REMEMBER, TOO THOSE
WHOSE SACRIFICES UNDERLIE THESE BLESSINGS

To the right of this block stands another granite block with the date 1975 inscribed. To the right of this block stands another large pole holding the United States flag. This completes the circular formation of the memorial.

WILLIAM WATSON MONUMENT (MEXICAN WAR VETERANS MONUMENT)

Location: Mount Royal Terrace and North Avenue
Designer: Edward Berge
Erected: 1903

The Maryland Association of Veterans of the Mexican War erected this monument as a tribute to Lieutenant Colonel William H. Watson (1808–1846) and fellow Marylanders who served and died in the Mexican-American War (1846–48). Watson, a former member of the Baltimore City Council and Speaker of the Maryland House of Delegates, commanded "Baltimore's Own," an infantry battalion during the war. He was killed in 1846 while leading a charge during the Battle of Monterey.

In 1894, the association received a $3,000 appropriation from the state legislature to assist it in erecting a monument in honor of Watson.[197] It soon became apparent, however, that additional funds would be needed. The state legislature helped again by passing an enabling act in 1896, giving the Baltimore city government authority to appropriate $5,000 to the cause.[198] The supplemental $5,000 was approved in 1902 by the mayor and city council of Baltimore.[199]

The association commissioned Baltimore sculptor Edward Berge to create the monument, which was to occupy the triangle of land bounded by Fayette and Liberty Streets and Park Avenue. The municipal art commission approved Berge's design but considered it to be "too fine and elaborate for the downtown area."[200] As an alternate location, the association selected the intersection of Mount Royal Terrace and Lanvale Street, which did receive approval from the municipal art commission.[201]

Construction was nearly complete in the spring of 1903 when the association ran out of money, and the planned May 30 dedication had to be postponed. In June 1903, with a deficit of $800 and unable to obtain additional funds, the veterans boxed up the unfinished work. It was to be a temporary situation until the financial problems were alleviated. However, the action brought the veterans into a dispute with the park board, which insisted that the boxing be removed.[202] Louis F. Beeler, president of the Maryland Mexican War Veterans Association, sent a letter to the board of park commissioners stating that because it was situated on a street and not in a public park, the park board had no authority in the matter. The park board subsequently replied with a letter emphasizing that the city charter

William Watson Monument/Mexican War Veterans Monument, Mount Royal Terrace and North Avenue. *Photo by author.*

gave it supervision over all monuments in the city and inquired as to when the boxing would be removed.[203]

After a lapse of one week, and with the boxing still in place, the park board contacted the city solicitor requesting an opinion as to the legality of ordering the removal of the boxing. City Solicitor W. Cabell Bruce stated that the park board did have the power to remove the boxing from the monument. Bruce's opinion stated, "That after giving reasonable notice to the association, the board would have the power to insist that the boxing should either be removed from the monument, or the monument itself, taken down and removed; and if the boxing was not then removed, I think that the board would have the power to take down the monument and remove it."[204]

By the third week in September 1903, the veterans were able to remove the boxing and complete the monument. The dedication exercises were held on September 21, 1903, the anniversary of the Battle of Monterey and the death of William Watson. Surviving veterans of the Mexican-American War and invited guests were seated on a stand in front of the monument.

The exercises opened with an invocation by Reverend William M. Dane. President Louis F. Beeler of the Maryland Mexican War Veterans Association presented the monument to Mayor Robert McLane, who accepted it on behalf of the city. Former congressman Charles R. Schirm and Democratic candidate for governor Edwin Warfield each delivered an address. Mrs. Monterey Watson Iglehart, daughter of William Watson, pulled aside the American flag covering the monument. She was born on the day that her father was killed. The flag was the same one draped over Watson's coffin when his body was brought home from Mexico.[205]

In the fall of 1936, the monument was moved to the intersection of Mount Royal Terrace and North Avenue, as selected by the municipal art commission. The relocation was necessary because of the Howard Street extension plan, which called for an underpass at the intersection of Mount Royal Terrace and Lanvale Street, and engineers feared that the weight of the monument would be too great for the structure beneath it.[206]

The ten-foot-high bronze statue of Watson surmounts a pedestal of Maryland granite twenty-two feet high. The statue depicts Watson with a drawn sword at his side and dressed in the uniform of an American Army officer during the Mexican-American War. The pedestal consists of a circular base, with the lowest step separated by two mounts on opposite sides with Mexican mortars. The shaft of the pedestal is of pilasters of modified Corinthian-style finished by an ornamental cornice and cap. On the side of the shaft there is a bronze dedicatory tablet. The name "WATSON" in bronze is attached to the front of the shaft just below the statue.

The inscription on the front of the tablet reads:

MEMORIAL
TO
MARYLANDERS
KILLED IN
WAR WITH MEXICO
1846–7-8
ERECTED BY THE
MARYLAND
ASSOCIATION OF VETERANS
OF THE MEXICAN WAR
1903

The inscription on the back tablet reads:

KILLED IN BATTLE:
LIEUT. COL. WILLIAM H. WATSON
MAJOR SAMUEL RINGGOLD
CAPT. RANDOLPH RIDGELY
CAPT. JAMES BOYD
LIEUT. JAMES TANEYHILL
SERGT. JOHN TRUSCOTT
PRIVATE GEORGE A. HERRING
PRIVATE ALEXANDER RAMSEY
PRIVATE JOSEPH WHARRY
PRIVATE PATRICK O'BRIEN
PRIVATE WM. J. ALEXANDER
PRIVATE WILLIAM CAPLAN
PRIVATE WILLIAM KELLY
PRIVATE WILLIAM REESE
PRIVATE JOHN R. RUSSELL

The inscription on the side tablet reads:

ASSOCIATION OF
THE VETERANS OF THE
MEXICAN WAR

MONUMENT COMMITTEE
1890–1903
LOUIS F. BEELER, PRESIDENT
JOSHUA LYNCH, VICE-PRESIDENT
JOHN F. FURY, VICE-PRESIDENT
HENRY BOWERS, VICE-PRESIDENT
GEORGE A. FREBURGER, MARSHAL
JAMES D. IGLEHART, SURGEON
JOHN D. ONION, SECRETARY
DECEASED
JOSEPH H. RUDDACH, PRESIDENT
WILLIAM LEE, VICE-PRESIDENT
JOHN T. GRAY, MARSHAL
WILLIAM LOUIS SCHLEY, SECRETARY
JOHN E. GOULD, SECRETARY
DAVID G. MURRAY, TREASURER

The inscription on the other side tablet reads:

ASSOCIATION OF
THE VETERANS OF THE
MEXICAN WAR
1846–7-8
SURVIVING MEMBERS
1903
OF THE ARMY:
JOHN A. REESE
SAMUEL C. LOVE
JOHN CAPENTER
ROBERT HARRINGTON
JOHN A. GALLOWAY
JOHN D. PRESTON
GEORGE W. BALL
OF THE NAVY:
WILLIAM H. JENKINS
WILLIAM WILLIAMS
ALEXANDER WILKINSON
HENRY W. TILSON
WILLIAM TAYLOR
CHARLES HILL
DAVID W. MERRIKEN
THOMAS P. RUSSELL

Chapter 9

PUBLIC SERVANTS

BALTIMORE CITY FIREFIGHTERS MEMORIAL

Location: Lexington and Gay Streets
Designer: Tylden Streett
Erected: 1990

Baltimore City established a paid fire department in 1858. Since that time, thousands of firefighters have served protecting the lives and property of the city. In doing so, many have lost their lives in the performance of their duties.

Plans for a memorial honoring the firefighters of Baltimore originated after the devastating Hochschild Kohn Department Store fire on February 17, 1983. Shortly after the fire, Roy Kirby, a successful building contractor, approached fire department officials about a proposal to honor the city's firefighters. As a result, a committee was formed in January 1984 to explore the possibility of erecting a memorial to Baltimore's firefighters, past, present and future. The committee consisted of honorary chairpersons Mayor William Donald Schaefer, Louis Grasmick and John Steadman; Peter J. O'Connor, chair; Herbert W. Catterton; Jeffrey Delistle; Patrick P. Flynn; Milton R. Jones; Roman Kaminski; Roy F. Kirby Sr.; Francis W. Kuchta; Fred Lazarus III; Warren Miller; Robert P. Mittelman; Charles "Bucky" Muth; Arnold Reynolds; John E. Roberts; and John L. Seiss.

Baltimore City Firefighters Memorial, Lexington and Gay Streets. *Photo by author.*

After numerous discussions on the virtues of a statue or memorial-type structure, the committee agreed on a statue of a firefighter in action. They further agreed to place the statue on the grounds of fire department headquarters at Lexington and Gay Streets.

On July 2, 1984, the committee announced a design competition to select a sculptor, with preference given (but not restricted) to Maryland artists. Of the eleven designs submitted by the deadline of October 1, 1984, they selected the entry submitted by Tylden Streett of the Maryland Institute College of Art.[207] Contributions from active and retired firefighters, the business community and the public covered the $107,000 cost.

The unveiling of the Baltimore City Firefighters Memorial occurred on April 19, 1990, at fire department headquarters, Gay and Lexington Streets. Attendees included Maryland governor William Donald Schaefer, Mayor Kurt Schmoke, city council president Mary Pat Clark and fire board commissioner David L. Glenn. Reverend Frank Bourbon, a fire department chaplain, delivered a dedicatory prayer. Peter J. O'Connor, chief of the fire department, delivered the main address. A third fire department chaplain, Reverend James Ball, gave the closing benediction.[208]

The inscription on the pedestal reads:

DEDICATED TO THE MEMBERS OF
THE BALTIMORE CITY FIRE DEPARTMENT
PAST PRESENT AND FUTURE

BALTIMORE CITY POLICE OFFICERS MEMORIAL

Location: Shot Tower Park, Fayette Street and the Fallsway
Designer: Unknown
Erected: 1978

The Baltimore City Police Department erected this memorial in recognition of the contributions made by the city's police officers dating back to 1794, as well as the establishment of the department. The memorial is in historic Shot Tower Park, on land that was once the residence of Baltimore's second mayor, Thorowgood Smith.

On June 24, 1978, members of the police department and citizens of the community attended the dedication of the memorial by Police Commissioner Donald Pomerleau. Mayor William Donald Schaefer and other government officials were in attendance. Thomas J. Keyes, a former deputy police commissioner, delivered a short address. A police officer and Boy Scout honor guard participated in the ceremony, which also included a performance by an army fife and drum corps.[209]

Baltimore City Police Officers Memorial, Shot Tower Park, Fayette Street and the Fallsway. *Photo by author.*

The memorial consists of three figurative statues, including two police officers standing and behind them a kneeling, grief-stricken police officer and child on a round base. A dedicatory bronze tablet mounted on a gray granite wall marks the center point of the memorial. The colorful emblem of the Baltimore City Police Department is located on each side of the tablet.

The inscription on the bronze tablet reads:

BALTIMORE POLICE DEPARTMENT
ESTABLISHED 1794

BY AN ACT OF THE MARYLAND LEGISLATURE
THIS LIVING MEMORIAL IS DEDICATED BY THE DEPARTMENT
TO ALL MEMBERS, PAST AND PRESENT, WHO HAVE SERVED
WITH HONOR, DEDICATION, AND LOYALTY, MANY OF WHOM
HAVE MADE THE SUPREME SACRIFICE
THEIR ACHIEVEMENT AND CONTRIBUTIONS HAVE ENHANCED THE
DEPARTMENT'S STATURE AND WELL-BEING OF THE
COMMUNITY THEY SERVE

DEDICATED 1978
DONALD D. POMERLEAU
POLICE COMMISSIONER

MERCHANT MARINE MEMORIAL

Location: Light Street and Key Highway
Designer: Ann Dudrow
Erected: 1979

Baltimore, with its rich maritime history, erected this memorial in honor of those men and women of the U.S. Merchant Marine who died in the service to their country. Funds to erect the memorial were provided by the National Maritime Union of America, the Seafarer's International Union, District 1 of the Pacific Coast Marine Engineers Beneficial Association (MEBA), the International Organization of Masters, Mates and Pilots and the Propeller Club of the Port of Baltimore.

Mayor William Donald Schaefer and Shannon J. Wall, president of the National Maritime Union of America, dedicated the memorial on May 22, 1979. A concert given by the Bay City Brass Band highlighted the ceremony.[210]

Merchant Marine Memorial, Light Street and Key Highway. *Photo by author.*

The six-foot square base was designed by Ann Dudrow of the architectural firm R.T.K.L. Associates. The granite slab is one foot in height, and the anchor which rests on it is made of iron. A bronze tablet is embedded into the granite slab just below the anchor, which was donated by Captain James M. Fesmire Jr. The insignia of the U.S. Merchant Marine is inscribed at the top of the tablet.

The inscription on the bronze tablet reads:

> To the memory
> United States Merchant Seamen
> who lost their lives serving
> the United States of America
> Donations: National Maritime Union of America
> International Organization of Master, Mates, and Pilots
> Seamens International Union of North America
> District 1 Pacific Coast District M.E.B.A.
> Propeller Club of the U.S. Port of Baltimore
> Anchor: Capt. James M. Fesmire, Jr.

Chapter 10

RELIGIOUS LEADERS

JAMES CARDINAL GIBBONS MEMORIAL

Location: Basilica of the Assumption grounds, Cathedral and Mulberry Streets
Designer: Betti Richard
Erected: 1967

Citizens of different faiths erected this memorial in honor of James Cardinal Gibbons (1834–1921), a man once described by the *New York Times* as "one of the wisest men in the world." Cardinal Gibbons was one of the most admired Baltimoreans and a friend and counselor to the wealthy and poor alike.

For forty years after his death, the citizens of Baltimore considered the idea of erecting a memorial to Cardinal Gibbons. In October 1963, a nonsectarian group of more than fifty influential Marylanders formed the Cardinal Gibbons Memorial Committee. Leonard A. Siems of Maryland National Bank and Joseph Healy, a prominent Catholic lay leader, served as co-chairpersons. The committee started a fundraising effort to obtain the anticipated $100,000 cost and secured the services of New York sculptor Betti Richard.[211]

Richard initially designed a seated figure of Gibbons cast in bronze and surrounded by a series of stone panels depicting episodes in the cardinal's career. However, when Richard learned that he habitually walked around

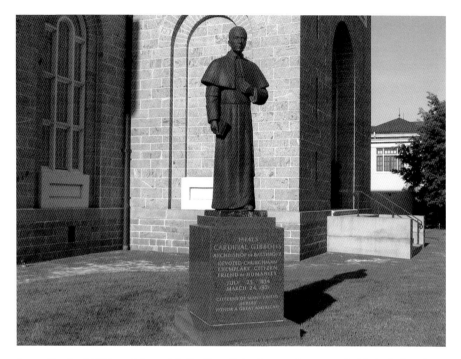

James Cardinal Gibbons Memorial, Basilica of the Assumption grounds, Cathedral and Mulberry Streets. *Photo by author.*

the city talking with people, she scaled back the design and changed it to a standing figure.[212] The cost was reduced as well to $40,000.

According to the original site plans, the new park being established at North Charles and Saratoga Streets was to be the location for the memorial. This was not possible, however, because of aesthetic considerations.[213] The location was subsequently changed to the Basilica of the Assumption grounds at Cathedral and Mulberry Streets.

More than two hundred persons, including the sculptor, Betti Richard, attended the dedication of the James Cardinal Gibbons Memorial on December 17, 1967. Leonard A. Siems presided over the exercises, which included tributes by Lawrence Cardinal Shehan, Rabbi Abraham Shusterman of Har Sinai Congregation and Reverend Paul E. Warren, pastor of the Second Presbyterian Church. Right Reverend Noble V. Powell, retired Episcopal bishop of Maryland, delivered the invocation. A group of four young schoolgirls unveiled the statue.[214]

The bronze statue is seven feet, six inches in height and depicts a standing Cardinal Gibbons gazing outward. His left hand rests on a pectoral cross, while his right hand holds a prayer book. The statue is situated on a pink granite pedestal four feet, six inches in height.

The inscription on the pedestal reads:

JAMES
CARDINAL GIBBONS
ARCHBISHOP OF BALTIMORE
DEVOTED CHURCHMAN
EXEMPLARY CITIZEN
FRIEND OF HUMANITY
JULY 23, 1834
MARCH 24, 1921

CITIZENS OF MANY FAITHS
HEREBY
HONOR A GREAT AMERICAN

MARTIN LUTHER MONUMENT

Location: East 32ⁿᵈ Street and Lake Montebello Drive
Designers: Hans Schuler and William W. Emmart
Erected: 1936

Arthur Wallenhorst, a devout Lutheran and successful Baltimore merchant, erected this monument in honor of Martin Luther (1483–1546), the patriarch of his church and leader of the Protestant Reformation. It is the first American-made statue of Luther, others being recasts from originals in Germany.

When Baltimore jeweler Arthur Wallenhorst died in 1933, he bequeathed $50,000 in his will for a monument to be erected in honor of Martin Luther. The will stipulated that it should have the inscription "Given by a Baltimore Jeweler." The trustees of the Luther Monument Bequest Fund selected noted Baltimore sculptor Hans Schuler to do the work. The trustees included George W. Livingston, chairperson; Harry C. Mueller; Peter E. Tome; Fritz O. Evers; and Martin Luther Enders.

A plot of land on Mount Royal Terrace near the entrance to Druid Hill Park was donated by the city government and approved by the municipal art commission.[215] Schuler studied contemporary portraits of Luther before beginning his work and used the works of the German Renaissance painter Lucas Cranach as a model.

The Martin Luther Monument was dedicated on October 31, 1936, with more than eight thousand people in attendance. The police band led three thousand Sunday school children from the Fifth Regiment Armory to the site. The exercises opened with the singing of "The Star-Spangled Banner," followed by an invocation given by Reverend Paul J. Mackensen, pastor of St. Paul's Lutheran Church. The Capella Chorus of Gettysburg College sang several hymns. Mayor Howard Jackson received the monument on behalf of the city and gave a short address. Eva Marie Luther, a descendant of Martin Luther and daughter of German ambassador Hans Luther, unveiled the statue.

During the unveiling, the municipal band played the "Hallelujah Chorus" from Handel's *Messiah*. Reverend Dr. O. Fritz Evers, pastor of Zion Church, made a brief address in German and then introduced Ambassador Luther, who gave a short address. The main speaker was Dr. Charles M. Jacobs, president of the Lutheran Theological Seminary of Philadelphia. Two wreaths were placed at the base of the monument, one from Martin Luther's birthplace, with a ribbon bearing a swastika, and one from Zion Church. "A Mighty Fortress Is Our God," was sung by the crowd. The closing

Martin Luther Monument, East 32nd Street and Lake Montebello Drive. *Photo by author.*

benediction was given by Reverend Dr. Martin Luther Enders, pastor of the First English Lutheran Church.[216]

When planning began on the Jones Falls Expressway in 1957, it became apparent that relocation of the monument would be necessary. The city proposed relocating it to park property at the north side of the 29th Street bridge near Sisson Street. This, however, met with strong opposition from the Lutheran Church. A compromise was reached, and it was moved to its present location in August 1959.

The Martin Luther Monument stands thirty-four feet above the ground. It consists of a large statue of Luther weighing nearly five tons and standing eighteen feet in height. The statue depicts Luther dressed in a religious robe with his right hand raised and giving a blessing, while his left hand clutches a prayer book against his chest. The pedestal on which the statue rests is twelve feet in height. The curved stone base is made of pink granite from Maine, sixty-two feet in width and thirty-five feet in depth. William W. Emmart designed the architectural setting. The Baltimore firm of Ruhlman and Wilson did the stonework. The statue was cast at the Roman Bronze Works of Corona, New York.

The inscription on the pedestal reads:

> Martin Luther
> Given by a Baltimore Jeweler

The inscription reads:

> "A Mighty Fortress Is Our God"

Pope John Paul II Memorial

Location: Basilica of the Assumption grounds, North Charles and Franklin Streets
Designer: Joseph Sheppard
Erected: 2008

Serving as the centerpiece of a beautiful garden on the grounds of Baltimore's Basilica of the Assumption stands a bronze life-size statue of Pope John Paul II (1920–2005). The sculptor, Joseph Sheppard, created it at his studio in Pietrasanta, Italy. Sheppard's inspiration came after seeing a photograph of

Pope John Paul II Memorial, Basilica of the Assumption grounds, North Charles and Franklin Streets. *Photo by author.*

the pontiff embracing two young children during his visit to Baltimore on October 8, 1995. The $1.3 million garden was funded by private donations.

Dedication of the Pope John Paul II Prayer Garden occurred on October 23, 2008, attended by approximately 150 people. Soprano Beverly Williams sang "Ave Maria" to open the ceremony. Cardinal William H. Keeler gave the opening blessing. William H. Borders, former head of the Archdiocese of Baltimore, also participated in the ceremony. Stephen Kelly of landscape architects Mahan Rykiel Associates, the firm that created the design for the garden, said that Sheppard's statue "aptly caught the pope's tenderness for children" and pointed out to the stone tablet engraved with the symbols of Judaism, Islam and Christianity to show the ecumenical beliefs of Pope John Paul II. Scott Rykiel, the principal architect of the garden, said, "We tried to make it a garden, rather than a plaza....We realized Pope John Paul II was an outdoorsman. He loved hiking in the mountains." Archbishop Edwin O'Brien and Joseph Sheppard unveiled the bronze likeness of the pontiff. Beverly Williams closed the ceremony by singing "Amazing Grace."[217]

The bronze figure of John Paul II is seven feet in height and weighs 850 pounds. It depicts him embracing two young children, a boy and a girl, and rests on a polished granite base. A large granite wall faces the statue with stainless steel bands embedded bearing the symbols of Christianity, Islam and Judaism. Concrete pillars hold the seal of Baltimore and the coat of arms of Pope John Paul II. The garden features plants, shrubs and trees specifically chosen for their relation to the Bible and Pope John Paul II.

The inscription on the base reads:

JOHANNES PAULUS P.P. II
October 16, 1978–April 2, 2005
KAROL JOZEF WOJTYLA
May 18, 1920–April 2, 2005

Chapter 11

SOCIAL REFORMERS

FREDERICK DOUGLASS MONUMENT

Location: Morgan State University Campus, Hillen Road and Cold Spring Lane
Designer: James E. Lewis
Erected: 1956

Located in front of Holmes Hall on the Morgan State University campus stands a bronze statue of the famous African American abolitionist, social reformer and statesman Frederick Douglass (1817–1895). When it was dedicated in 1956, it was the first monument erected to Douglass in Maryland, his native state.

The idea of a statue honoring Frederick Douglass was first proposed in 1943 by George C. Grant, president of the Maryland Education Association, an organization of Black teachers. The idea was well received, and to raise funds, an appeal was made to the schoolchildren of Maryland. Pennies, nickels and dimes slowly accumulated, and with the assistance of parent-teachers associations and other clubs, the necessary $10,000 goal was achieved.[218]

John E. Lewis, head of the art department at Morgan State University, submitted an eighteen-inch sketch of Douglass after being invited to do so by the association. Officials of the association were favorably impressed by the sketch and gave Lewis the commission.[219] Lewis worked for two years to get the right spirit into the statue. He made several trips to the home of Frederick Douglass in Anacostia, where he studied death masks and photographs of the abolitionist.

Frederick Douglass
Monument, Morgan
State University
Campus, Hillen Road
and Cold Spring Lane.
Photo by author.

Dedication of the Frederick Douglass Monument was held on October 20, 1956, the culmination of a thirteen-year project. Former Maryland governor Theodore McKeldin officiated at the ceremony and delivered a short speech.

Historian Benjamin A. Quarles, a Douglass biographer, delivered the main address. Student representatives from every Maryland county and Baltimore City unveiled the statue.[220]

The bronze statue, which measures eight feet, four inches in height, depicts an elderly Douglass in a walking posture. He is bareheaded and dressed in a frock coat. In his right hand, he carries the cane presented to him by Mary Todd Lincoln. The four-foot-high pedestal cost $8,000 and was provided by the State of Maryland.

The inscriptions on the pedestal read:

[FRONT]
FREDERICK DOUGLASS
1817–1895
HUMANITARIAN
STATESMAN

[BACK]
ERECTED
BY THE
MARYLAND EDUCATION
ASSOCIATION

THROUGH CONTRIBUTIONS OF
CHILDREN IN COLORED SCHOOLS
AND CITIZENS OF MARYLAND
IN THE YEAR
1956

"I AM AN AMERICAN
AND AS AN AMERICAN
I SPEAK FOR AMERICA"
FREDERICK DOUGLASS

JOHN E. LEWIS, SCULPTOR

FREDERICK DOUGLASS MONUMENT

Location: Frederick Douglass–Isaac Myers Maritime Park, Fells Point
Designer: Marc Andre Robinson
Erected: 2006

Located in front of the Frederick Douglass–Isaac Myers Maritime Park
in historic Fells Point stands a large bronze bust of the famous abolitionist
Frederick Douglass (1817–1895). The park celebrates the contributions of

Frederick Douglass
Monument, Frederick
Douglass–Isaac Myers
Maritime Park, Fells Point.
Photo by author.

African Americans in the development of Baltimore's maritime industry. Douglass worked as a slave in the shipyards of Fells Point before escaping to freedom in 1838. The sculpture by Marc Andre Robinson, a Maryland Institute College of Art graduate, stands six feet tall and wide and weighs 1,100 pounds.

GEORGE PEABODY MONUMENT

Location: Mount Vernon Place
Designer: William Wetmore Story
Erected: 1890

Wealthy Baltimore businessman, banker and international philanthropist George Peabody (1795–1869) is honored by this bronze likeness of him located in Mount Vernon Place, near the institute that bears his name. Peabody was known for his generosity and is regarded as the "Father of Modern Philanthropy."

Peabody's charitable activities were aimed toward improving society. He founded and financially supported numerous institutions, including the Peabody Institutes in Baltimore and Massachusetts, his native state. After moving to London, England, in 1837, he established the Peabody Donation Fund, which provided subsidized housing for the working class.

The George Peabody Monument is a life-size bronze statue depicting him seated in a relaxed pose with his legs crossed. It rests on a granite

George Peabody Monument, Mount Vernon Place. *Photo by author.*

166

pedestal approximately five feet in height. It is a replica of a bronze statue made for the city of London by William Wetmore Story, who has been called "the most cultured and perhaps most academic of America's early sculptors." The London statue was unveiled by the Prince of Wales in 1869, just a few months before the death of Peabody. Baltimore's copy was presented to the city as a gift from Robert Garrett, president of the Baltimore and Ohio Railroad.

Dedication of the George Peabody Monument occurred on April 7, 1890. In presenting the statue to the city, Robert Garrett stated in a letter to Mayor Robert Davidson, "It has seemed to me appropriate that our city should contain some memorial to George Peabody to whose munificence it is indebted."[221]

The inscription on a bronze tablet on the front of the pedestal reads:

GEORGE PEABODY
1795–1869

The inscription on a bronze tablet on the back of the pedestal reads:

THIS STATUE WAS PRESENTED TO
THE CITY OF BALTIMORE
APRIL 7, 1890
BY ROBERT GARRETT
1847–1896
PRESIDENT OF
THE BALTIMORE AND OHIO RAILROAD
1884–1887

JAMES RIDGELY MONUMENT

Location: Harlem Park, Edmondson Avenue and Gilmore Street
Designer: Michael Muldoon
Erected: 1885

In 1885, four years after the death of James L. Ridgely (1807–1881), the Independent Order of Odd Fellows erected this monument in his honor. He was a distinguished member of the organization, which had its American origins in Baltimore. In addition to holding many posts

James Ridgely Monument, Harlem Park, Edmondson Avenue and Gilmore Street. *Photo by author.*

within the organization, Ridgely also held many Baltimore and Maryland government positions.

Shortly after his death, a plan to erect a monument in honor of Ridgely in Baltimore was suggested by John L. Smith, an Odd Fellow member from Connecticut. A nationwide fundraising effort was established for the project, soliciting five-cent subscriptions. Odd Fellow member and former Baltimore mayor Joshua Vansant administered the fund until 1883, when Sovereign Lodge, in session at Providence, Rhode Island, appointed a committee to take charge of the fund. Michael Muldoon, a designer from Kentucky, was commissioned at a cost of $30,000 to create the monument. In 1884, the city council passed a resolution authorizing the use of Harlem Square as a location.[222]

A cornerstone laying ceremony was held on April 27, 1885, preceded by a small parade. The Fifth Regiment Band and the Encampment Drill Association led the way, followed by the marshals and members of several state grand lodges in their carriages. According to a local newspaper account, "The procession, though small, made a good impression, the flashing swords and purple plumes and the rich banners of the drill association, and the many colored, artistically embroidered regalia of the various officers forming bright, pleasant contrasts."[223]

The procession moved along the streets from Odd Fellows Hall on Gay Street to Harlem Park. At the west side of the park, the grand officers occupied seats on the platform. Grand Sire Henry F. Garey made a short address, and a list of articles being placed into the cornerstone was read by Grand Secretary Theodore A. Ross. Into the copper box, twelve inches long, six inches wide and six inches deep, he laid copies of the *Baltimore Sun* newspaper and other daily and weekly journals, the journal of the Foreign Grand Lodge of the Independent Order of Odd Fellows for the years 1881 through 1884, the journal of the Grand Lodge of Maryland for 1884 and 1885, circulars and proclamations relating to the death of James Ridgely and the construction of the monument, a program for the celebration of the sixty-sixth anniversary of the Order of the Grand Lodge of Maryland, order of procession and exercises at the laying of the cornerstone, a small box containing coins of the United States in 1885 and a list of contributors to the monument.

Grand Sire Garey placed the box into the northeast corner of the base, saying, "In the name of friendship as pure as the water, I lay this stone." He then sprinkled water three times on the stone from a vessel handed to him by the deputy grand sire. "In love, symbolized by these flowers, I lay this cornerstone," he stated as he tossed roses and lilies from a wreath handed to him by the grand chaplain. "In truth, represented by this wheat, I lay this cornerstone," he remarked while tossing wheat from a silver vessel. He then proceeded to strike the stone three times with a gavel, stating as he did so, "In benevolence and charity I lay this cornerstone." He then laid cement on the stone and stated to the crowd, "This cornerstone duly laid according to regular and ancient form, and the shaft is to rise upon it consecrated to the memory of James L. Ridgely." The ceremonies concluded with a prayer and an announcement that completion of the monument was expected by September 21 of that year.[224]

The Ridgely Monument was completed as scheduled, with the dedication occurring on September 22, 1885. This ceremony was also proceeded by a small parade of Odd Fellows from several East Coast state lodges and encampments. Dignitaries of the Odd Fellows, seated in their carriages, led the way. The parade traveled from Gay Street to the monument site in Harlem Park. In passing city hall, the parade was reviewed by Maryland governor Henry Lloyd, Mayor Ferdinand Latrobe and members of the city council. Large crowds gathered on both sides of the street along the parade route.

At the site, an estimated fifteen thousand people were assembled around the platform. The grand officers of the order were escorted to their seats on the platform by the grand marshal and his staff. The monument committee occupied seats next to them, followed by Mayor Latrobe and the city council. John J. Gallagher of Delaware, secretary of the monument committee, presented the monument to the Sovereign Grand Lodge. In his remarks, he thanked the City of Baltimore and specifically the park board for donating the land. After Gallagher finished his remarks, architect Michael Muldoon released the cover from the statue of Ridgely. Grand Sire Henry F. Garey accepted the monument on behalf of all Odd Fellows and gave a speech praising the life of James Ridgely. A closing benediction was given by Grand Chaplain Reverend J.W. Venable, an Episcopal minister from Kentucky.[225]

The James Ridgely Monument is constructed of Vermont granite and is forty feet in height. It is topped by the bronze statue of Ridgely seven feet, three inches in height. He is depicted holding a scroll in his right hand and looking to the east. It has an ornate Gothic base of three granite blocks, a plinth, a die-block decorated with columns and arches and a second block that ends in the pedestal of the statue. Four bronze medallions are located on the base bearing the seal of the Grand Lodge, with an "all-seeing-eye" above it. The entire monument weighs 170 tons.

The inscription on the base reads:

[EAST SIDE]
I.O.O.F.
FRIENDSHIP LOVE AND TRUTH

JAMES L. RIDGELY
BORN JANUARY 27, 1808
DIED NOVEMBER 16, 1881
FLT

[WEST SIDE]
INITIATED IN COLUMBIA LODGE NO. 6, BALTIMORE, MAY 1829
INITIATED IN JERUSALEM ENCAMPMENT NO. 1, BALTIMORE,
MARCH 5, 1830
GRAND SECRETARY OF GRAND LODGE OF MARYLAND, JANUARY 29,

1834
GRAND SECRETARY OF GRAND LODGE OF THE UNITED STATES
APRIL 24, 1840

[NORTH SIDE]
A LEGISLATOR FOR HIS CITY AND STATE
A PERSON OF EDUCATION
AND A REPRESENTATIVE AMERICAN CITIZEN

[SOUTH SIDE]
NOR MARBLE NOR BRASS CAN BE SO ENDURING
A MONUMENT AS THE MEMORY OF HIS
NAME, AND HIS DEEDS
GRATEFUL TO HIS CREATOR
FAITHFUL TO HIS COUNTRY
FRATERNAL TO HIS FELLOW MAN
SUCH A LIFE ELEVATES AND EXALTS HUMAN NATURE

THOMAS WILDEY MONUMENT

Location: Broadway and Fayette Street
Designer: Edward F. Durrand
Erected: 1865

The Independent Order of Odd Fellows erected this monument as a tribute to Thomas Wildey (1782–1861), founder of this nonsectarian and benevolent organization. As a young immigrant to America living in Baltimore, Wildey found himself lonely and estranged from the residents of the city. In 1819, he formed the Independent Order of Odd Fellows in America and formed its first lodge. In addition to companionship, its main objective was to "relieve the distressed, bury the dead, and care for the widows and orphans." By the time of his death in 1861, there were lodges in forty-two states with more than 200,000 members.

Immediately after Wildey's death in 1861, the Grand Lodge of Maryland adopted a resolution calling for the construction of a monument in his honor. The resolution was sent to the Grand Lodge of the United States, hoping that lodges in other states would join the effort. The Grand Lodge of the United States, in turn, appointed a seven-member committee to receive drawings and designs for a monument and estimates of construction costs. A fundraising campaign was conducted, and by the end of 1864, more than $15,000 had been collected.[226]

At a session of the Grand Lodge of the United States held in Boston, Massachusetts, in September 1864, a design was adopted, and Baltimore was selected as the location. The design of Edward F. Durrand of Philadelphia was chosen, and he was contracted by the Odd Fellows to supervise the construction. The firms of Henry S. Tarr of Philadelphia and Bevan and Sons were hired to do the marble work.

At first, the Odd Fellows petitioned the board of park commissioners for approval to erect it in Druid Hill Park. The park board rejected the request, however, claiming that it was not the board's policy to allow monuments in the city parks honoring individuals.[227] The Odd Fellows then sought permission from the city government to erect it on Broadway, just north of Fayette Street. The mayor and city council agreed and donated the land.[228]

The cornerstone of the Thomas Wildey Monument was laid on April 26, 1865, preceded by a parade of Odd Fellows. The parade began at the Odd Fellows Hall on Gay Street and marched through the streets of the city to the monument site. A stand decorated with flags, banners and a large life-size portrait of Thomas Wildey was located at the site. Seated on the stand were the Grand Sire of the United States, officers and representatives of the Grand Lodge of Maryland and officers of the Grand Encampment.

The ceremony opened with a prayer by Reverend John McCron, acting Grand Chaplain, followed by an address from Grand Master Henry F. Garey. The cornerstone was then laid by Isaac M. Veitch of St. Louis, Missouri, Grand Sire of the United States. Inside the cornerstone, he placed a copper box, nineteen inches long, six inches wide and six inches deep. The box contained a eulogy of the life and character of Thomas Wildey by James L. Ridgely, proceedings of the Grand Lodge of Maryland on the death of Wildey, proceedings of the Grand Lodge of the United States on the same subject, proceedings of the organization of the Grand Lodge of Maryland, newspapers of the day, a record of the proceedings on laying the cornerstone, a copy of the ceremonies used on the occasion and several gold and silver American coins. The stone was then lifted in its place at the northeast angle of the base.

At this point, the Grand Sire poured water on the stone while saying, "In friendship I lay this stone, earnestly praying that while it remains its place among its fellows on this firm base, the brethren throughout our domain may be firmly bound in bonds fraternal." The building committee then

Thomas Wildey Monument, Broadway and Fayette Street. *Photo by author.*

handed a trowel to the Grand Sire, who spread mortar onto the stone. The ceremony concluded with a prayer by the Grand Chaplain.[229]

Completion of the monument occurred in September 1865 and was dedicated on September 20 with more than fifty thousand Odd Fellows in attendance. The occasion was significant because it brought together members from all over the country for the first time since the outbreak of the Civil War. The ceremony was preceded by a parade of Odd Fellows, taking the same route as did the one five months earlier for the laying of the cornerstone. Dignitaries of the order led four divisions in the parade. The event was a holiday in Baltimore, with most businesses closed.

Bands played as a huge crowd assembled around the monument. A stand set up nearby was occupied by local, state and federal officials; the Wildey Monument Committee; the Independent Blues Band; and officers of the Independent Order of Odd Fellows. Reverend J.D. Williamson, Grand Chaplain of the Grand Lodge of the United States, opened the ceremony with a prayer. A song written for the occasion by James R. Brewer of Baltimore was sung by a choir under the direction of James L. Camp. Joseph B. Escavaille, secretary of the Wildey Monument Committee, read a statement about the origin of the monument. At this point in the ceremony, Joseph Kidder, Grand Marshal of the Grand Lodge of the United States, along with John Q. Herrin, Grand Marshal of Maryland and his aides, Joshua Lynch and Robert King, performed the unveiling. Past sire James B. Nicholson formally presented the monument to the Grand Lodge of the United States, and it was accepted by Isaac M. Veitch, Grand Sire of the United States, with a short speech. A closing benediction was given by Reverend J.D. Williamson.[230]

The Thomas Wildey Monument stands on a base of rough granite, ten feet, six inches square, with its diagonal points setting truly with the points of a compass. From this rises the white marble base of the structure. On the four sides of the base block, carved in bas-relief, the produce of the North American continent is depicted, along with carved dedicatory inscriptions. Above this base or plinth is the pedestal, having on the southern face a bronze circular tablet with the seal of the Grand Lodge of the United States. Inscribed on the seal are these words: "Grand Lodge of the United States of the Independent Order of Odd fellows 1834. We command you to visit the sick, relieve the distressed, bury the dead, and educate the orphans."

On the eastern and western sides are circular bronze tablets on which are carved the figures of Faith and Hope. The northern side also contains a circular bronze tablet. Inscribed on this tablet are these words: "This column erected by the joint contributions of the lodges, encampments, and individual members of the Independent Order of Odd Fellows of the United States of America and jurisdiction thereunto belonging commemorates the founding of that order in the City of Baltimore on the 26th Day of April 1819 by Thomas Wildey."

The pedestal supports a full order of the Grecian Doric architecture. On the four sides of the frieze of tablets are carved the emblems of the order: the three links, the heart and hand, the bundle of rods and the globe. The order is surrounded by a life-size figure of Charity. She is cradling an orphan in her left arm, while another orphan stands at her right side. The entire monument stands fifty-two feet, seven inches in height.

The inscriptions on the base read:

> [NORTHEAST]
> THE SITE FOR THIS MONUMENT
> WAS UNANIMOUSLY VOTED BY
> THE MAYOR AND CITY COUNCIL
> OF BALTIMORE
> ANNO DOMINI
> MDCCCLXV
>
> [NORTHWEST]
> HE WHO REALIZES THAT
> THE TRUE MISSION OF
> MAN ON EARTH IS TO
> RISE ABOVE THE LEVEL
> OF INDIVIDUAL INFLUENCE
> AND TO RECOGNIZE THE
> FATHERHOOD OF GOD OVER
> ALL AND THE BROTHERHOOD
> OF MAN IS NATURE'S
> TRUE NOBLEMAN
>
> HENRY S. TARR, PHIL.
> BEVAN AND SONS, BALT.
>
> [SOUTHWEST]
> THOMAS WILDEY
> BORN JANUARY 15, 1782
>
> THOMAS WILDEY
> DIED OCTOBER 19, 1861

[SOUTHEAST]
THIS COLUMN
ERECTED BY THE JOINT
CONTRIBUTIONS OF THE LODGES
ENCAMPMENTS AND INDIVIDUAL
MEMBERS OF THE
INDEPENDENT ORDER OF ODD FELLOWS
OF THE
UNITED STATES OF AMERICA
AND
JURISDICTION THEREUNTO BELONG
COMMEMORATES
THE FOUNDING OF THAT ORDER IN
THE CITY OF BALTIMORE ON THE
26TH DAY OF APRIL 1819
BY
THOMAS WILDEY

Members of the Wildey Monument Committee:
James B. Nicholson, of Pennsylvania
John W. Stokes, of Pennsylvania
James L. Ridgely, of Maryland
James L. Escvaille, of Maryland
A.H. Ranson, of Kentucky
Theodore A. Ross, of New Jersey

Chapter 12

WAR HEROES

George Armistead Monument

Location: Federal Hill Park
Designer: Gotleib Mezger
Erected: 1882

Located on top of historic Federal Hill, across from Baltimore's Inner Harbor, stands a monument in honor of Colonel George Armistead (1780–1818), the "Hero of Fort McHenry." The city government erected the monument in 1882 as a replacement for a previous one that was accidently destroyed nineteen years earlier.

During the War of 1812, Colonel Armistead commanded Fort McHenry, which guarded the entrance to Baltimore's harbor. On September 13, 1814, the British navy attacked the fort. After a twenty-five-hour bombardment, they could not get close enough and withdrew. Armistead and the fort's garrison held off the attack, crushing British hopes of capturing the city. George Armistead died four years later at the age of thirty-nine.

In 1827, the relatives of George Armistead procured a monument to his memory and asked Mayor Jacob Small to find them a suitable location within the city to place it.[231] The mayor and city council subsequently authorized placement of it on a lot occupied by the Charles Street spring under the direction of the city commissioners.[232] It was later discovered, however, that the design was such that it could not stand in an unsupported position, and the location was changed to a niche in the keeper's house at the Calvert Street spring.[233]

In 1828, the niche received the marble monument, which contained the following inscription:

> Colonel George Armistead, in honor of whom this monument
> is erected, was the gallant defender of Fort McHenry during
> the bombardment of the British Fleet, 13th September 1814.
> He died universally esteemed and regretted on the 25th of April
> 1818, aged thirty-nine years.

A sketch of the first monument and its setting is included in Lossing's *Pictorial Book of the War of 1812* (New York, 1869). In the course of time, the spring fell into a dilapidated state, and during renovations in 1863, the monument was mistakenly carried away in the debris.[234]

In 1879, the city council passed a resolution appropriating $1,200 for the erection of another monument in honor of Armistead and appointed a committee of three council members to select a design and location for it.[235] After consulting with City Solicitor Thomas Hall, however, Mayor Ferdinand Latrobe vetoed the resolution.[236] Hall contended that the city charter provided no authority to erect the monument in his opinion. He stated that "unless the authority to do so can be shown to have been conferred by the state legislature, the question must be answered in the negative."[237] The city council failed in its attempt to override the veto.[238]

The Maryland General Assembly, during its 1880 session, enacted legislation granting the city government authority to erect the monument.[239] The city council subsequently passed the legislation again, with a $2,000 appropriation.[240] Mayor Latrobe vetoed this resolution as well, citing a shortage of funds in the city treasury.[241] The following year, 1882, brought a change in the administration of the Baltimore city government. The city again passed the resolution of a year earlier, which received the approval of the new mayor, William Pinkney Whyte.[242]

Dedication of the second monument to George Armistead occurred on September 12, 1882, at its location on Eutaw Place, between Wilson and Laurens Streets. A crowd of nearly five thousand people surrounded the covered stand, on which sat invited guests, government officials, monument committee members, a choir from the Baltimore Oratorio Society and the Wilson Point Band. Mayor Pinkney Whyte presided over the ceremony.

The exercises started with the band playing "Hail Columbia," followed by an opening prayer from Reverend Julius Grammar of St. Peter's Protestant Episcopal Church. The band played a rendition of the "Armistead March,"

George Armistead Monument, Federal Hill Park. *Photo by author.*

written for the occasion by Colonel James Deems. The monument, which had been covered by the American flag, was unveiled at this point. R. Stockett Matthews, a prominent Baltimore attorney, delivered a lengthy address, followed by the band playing "The Star-Spangled Banner." William C. Carter, chairman of the Armistead Monument Committee, recited a poem titled "The Bombardment of Fort McHenry," written by Professor J.H. Hewitt. The exercises concluded with the band playing "My Country, 'Tis of Thee" and "Stars and Stripes Forever."[243]

In 1886, the monument was moved to its present location on Federal Hill. The relocation was a result of protests from Eutaw Place residents who complained that the height did not harmonize with the loftiness of their homes.[244]

The Baltimore firm of Gotleib Mezger designed and constructed the monument of white marble. The design is a die-block fourteen feet high on a base eighteen inches high. Skyward-pointing cannons stand at each corner. On top of the block at each corner rests a cannonball. The cornice is surmounted by a flamed ball banded with stars. On the front side of the block are a carved sword and scabbard crossed, as well as a laurel wreath. Beneath is inscribed the name "COLONEL GEORGE ARMISTEAD."

The inscriptions on the monument read:

[Front]
This monument
is erected in honor of
the gallant defender
of Fort McHenry
near this city
during its
bombardment by
the British fleet
on the
13th and 14th September 1814
He died
universally esteemed
and regretted
on April 25th 1818
in the 25th year of his age

[Back]
Erected by
The mayor and city council
of Baltimore
Wm. Pinkney Whyte, Mayor
In pursuance of a resolution
approved May 3rd 1882
as a substitute for the monument
erected by a former mayor and city
council, in pursuance of resolutions
approved March 24th 1827
and February 4th 1828
which stood in the Calvert Street Spring
grounds until it became
defaced and destroyed by time
during the period of
thirty-five years
Esto Perpetuum!

[East Side]
Appointed Second Lieutenant of
The 7th Infantry, January 8th 1799
Appointed Ensign of Infantry
January 14th 1799
Appointed First Lieutenant of the
7th Infantry May 14th 1800
Transferred to the First Regiment
of Artillerists and Engineers
February 16th 1801
Appointed First Lieutenant in
the Regiment of Artillerists April
17th 1802
Appointed Assistant Military
Agent at Fort Niagara May—

[West Side]
Appointed Assistant Pay Master
February, 1806
Appointed Captain of Artillerists and
Engineers, November 1st 1806
Appointed Major of the 3rd Artillery
March 3rd 1814 for gallant services at
Fort George Upper Canada May 27th
1813. Transferred to the Artillery Corps
under the Act of March 30th 1814
Appointed Brevet Lieutenant Colonel September
20th 1814 for gallant services in defense
of Fort McHenry, to the rank as such from September
12th 1814

GEORGE ARMISTEAD MONUMENT

Location: Fort McHenry National Monument
Designer: Edward Berge
Erected: 1914

In commemoration of the 100th anniversary of the Battle of Baltimore and
the writing of "The Star-Spangled Banner" by Francis Scott Key, the City
of Baltimore held a celebration during the week of September 6–13, 1914.

George Armistead
Monument, Fort
McHenry National
Monument. *Photo by
author.*

As part of the festivities, the Star-Spangled Banner Centennial Commission
and the Society of the War of 1812 unveiled this bronze statue of Colonel
George Armistead inside Fort McHenry National Monument. Armistead
was the commanding officer of Fort McHenry during the bombardment of
the fort by the British navy on September 13, 1814. The attack was repelled,
and the city of Baltimore was saved from being captured by the British.

The dedication ceremony, which occurred on September 12, 1914,
included a 250-piece military band. Sixty thousand people attended the
event, including two hundred members of the Grand Army of the Republic.
Distinguished guests included Secretary of Labor William B. Wilson,
the governors of several states, Congressman J. Charles Linthicum and
descendants of Francis Scott Key and George Armistead. Secretary of State
William Jennings Bryan delivered the main address, followed by speeches
from Virginia governor Henry C. Stuart and Maryland governor Phillips
Lee Goldsborough. Dr. James Iglehart, president of the Maryland Chapter
of the Society of the War of 1812, presented the monument to Mayor James
Preston, who accepted it for the city. George Armistead, the great-grandson
of Colonel George Armistead, unveiled the statue.[245]

The bronze statue, created at a cost of $5,000, was created by Baltimore
artist Edward Berge.[246] Standing nine feet in height, the statue rests on a

granite pedestal thirteen feet, four inches in height. The figure of Armistead, dressed in the uniform of an American Army officer of 1812, is depicted gazing out over the waters of the Patapsco River.

The inscriptions on the pedestal read:

[Front]
ARMISTEAD

[Back]
JAMES H. PRESTON, MAYOR
PRESIDENT OF THE STAR-SPANGLED
BANNER CENTENNIAL COMMISSION
ARTHUR B. BIBBONS
CHAIRMAN
DR. JAMES IGLEHART
PRES. SOCIETY WAR OF 1812
JOHN A. WILSON
GEORGE ARMISTEAD
RICHARD H. SPENCER
EDWARD BERGE, SCULPTOR

[Left Side]
ERECTED SEPT. 12, 1914
BY THE CITY OF BALTIMORE
SOC. WAR OF 1812 CONTRIBUTING
IN COMMEMORATION OF THE GALLANT
DEFENSE OF FORT MCHENRY
UNDER THE COMMAND OF
COL. GEORGE ARMISTEAD
OF THE NATIONAL ANTHEM
THE STAR-SPANGLED BANNER

[Right Side]
COLONEL GEORGE ARMISTEAD
APRIL 10, 1799–APRIL 25, 1818
COMMANDER OF THIS FORT
DURING THE BOMBARDMENT
BY THE BRITISH FLEET
SEPT. 13–14, 1814, WAR OF 1812

BATTLE MONUMENT

Location: Fayette and Calvert Streets
Designers: Maximilian Godefroy and Antonio Capellano
Erected: 1815

Of all the monuments cast in bronze or carved in stone that grace the city of Baltimore, none is more revered than the Battle Monument. Erected in honor of the forty-two soldiers killed in the defense of Baltimore during the War of 1812, it is the first American-made war monument in the country. Located at the intersection of Fayette and Calvert Streets, known as Battle Monument Square and considered by many to be Baltimore's most historic spot, it stands on ground originally occupied by the city's first courthouse.

After the old courthouse was razed around 1808, the site was selected as the location for the proposed monument in honor of George Washington. When plans for the monument were adopted, however, the citizens became alarmed at the idea of having such a tall structure in the center of the city. This reaction necessitated changing the location of the Washington Monument to Howard's Hill, just north of the city limits.

Following the War of 1812, the citizens of Baltimore wanted to show their gratitude in some way to those soldiers who defended the city from the British attack on September 12–14, 1814. On March 1, 1815, the Committee of Vigilance and Safety, a citizens group that mobilized the city for defense, unanimously passed a resolution calling for the construction of a monument to honor those soldiers who died in the attack. Courthouse Square was selected as a location and received the necessary approval from the Maryland legislature during its 1815 session.[247]

To oversee fundraising and construction, a public subscription drive commenced on March 1, 1815, headed by a five-member committee consisting of James A. Buchanan, Samuel Hollingworth, Richard Frisby, Joseph Jamison and Henry Payson. Wanting to make the monument a general mark of admiration, the committee declined any subscription of more than $5 from any one individual. Mayor Edward Johnson, chairman of the Committee of Vigilance and Safety, made the first contribution. Poor and wealthy citizens alike made contributions. By this method, the committee raised $3,760.50. This amount proved to be insufficient, however, and the $5 limit was removed on July 14, 1815. Overall, the committee raised $10,000 through popular subscription from about 1,500 citizens.[248]

The Battle Monument Committee commissioned the French architect Maximilian Godefroy to design the monument. Godefroy submitted three designs, from which the committee selected the one that depicts it as it exists today.

A cornerstone laying ceremony was held on September 12, 1815, the first anniversary of the Battle of Baltimore. A parade from Great York Street (now Baltimore Street) to the site preceded the exercises. A scale model of the monument, created by John Finley and Rembrandt Peale, was carried through the streets on a cart drawn by six white horses. The Baltimore Independent Blues, consisting of men who had contributed one day's wages to the subscription fund, escorted the procession. All commercial activity in the city stopped for the day.

Upon arrival at the square, the band, under the direction of Professors Nensinger and Bunzie, played music selected for the occasion. Right Reverend Bishop Kent gave a prayer, after which Maximilian Godefroy—assisted by General Samuel Smith, General John Stricker, Colonel George Armistead and Mayor Edward Johnson—laid the cornerstone. Sealed in the cornerstone were several gold, silver and copper coins, along with a copy of the subscription book, newspapers of the previous day and a copper plate engraved with a dedicatory inscription. Reverend Dr. Inglis delivered an address, followed by a military salute in conjunction with the firing of several minute guns and the ringing of bells at Christ Church.[249]

In the fall of 1815, the Battle Monument Committee commissioned Antonio Capellano, formerly the First Sculptor to the Court of Madrid, to create a statue of Lady Baltimore to adorn the top. Capellano ordered marble from Italy and began work on his preliminary model. He soon faced a delay, however, when the ship carrying the marble encountered rough weather and docked in Malaga for repairs.[250] Meanwhile, Capellano continued work on his preliminary model. The marble eventually arrived, and Capellano commenced work on the statue.

By the end of 1816, work had progressed to the point that the pedestal reached the height of the cornice. The cornices arrived in April 1817 and the column in October of that year, when the cornices and the blocks forming the socle of the column were raised. Baltimore stonecutters John C. Neale, Frederick Baughman and Elias Hore performed the work.[251]

In an impressive ceremony on September 12, 1822, the finished statue of Lady Baltimore was placed on its pedestal surmounting the column. Prior to the ceremony, the Third and Fourteenth Brigades of Maryland Militia and the garrison from Fort McHenry formed a square around the monument.

Battle Monument, Fayette and Calvert Streets. *Photo by author.*

Generals Smith, Winder, Stricker and Stansbury occupied seats on a platform built for the occasion. Other dignitaries seated on the platform included veterans of the Revolutionary War and War of 1812, members of the Battle Monument Committee, the mayor and city council, members of the late Committee of Vigilance and Safety, judges and civil officers of the federal and state governments and officers of the army and navy. James Mosher Jr. delivered the main address, after which the marble statue was hoisted from the ground and placed on the pedestal while the military fired a salute.[252]

Completion of the monument occurred in December 1825, taking nearly ten years. Because of rising costs, it became necessary for the city council to appropriate money as needed, contributing approximately $21,000 over the ten-year period.[253] In 1827, the city government adopted the Battle Monument for use on the official city seal.[254]

The Battle Monument stands on a pedestal measuring four feet in height and forty feet on each side. Situated above the pedestal is an Egyptian-style tomb consisting of eighteen layers of stone, representing the eighteen states in the Union in 1815. On each of the four sides of the tomb is a false door, formed of a single slab of black marble, giving the impression that the dead are buried within, the whole forming what is known as a cenotaph. The doors are reached by ascending three steps intended to indicate the three years of the war. At the top is a cornice with griffins (animals with lion bodies and eagle heads) on each of the four corners. Between these are winged globes, representing eternity and the wings of time, which flies.

The column, supported by a square base, is in the form of fasces (bundles of rods and axe), signifying the strength of the Union. Binding the fasces of the column are fillets inscribed with the names of the thirty-nine enlisted men killed in defense of the city. Four bas-reliefs are located at the foot of the column. On the north face, a scene depicts the fighting at North Point, and on the south face, a scene depicts the bombardment of Fort McHenry, the two skirmishes during the Battle of Baltimore. On the east and west sides are lachrymal urns, emblems of regret and tears. At the top of the column are two wreaths, one of laurel expressing glory and the other of cypress expressing sorrow. The names of the three officers killed are engraved between the two wreaths. The combined height of the tomb and column is thirty-nine feet, which is symbolic of the year 1815 and the thirty-ninth year of American independence.

Surmounting the column is the statue of Lady Baltimore, her head bearing a mural crown. The figure, which is nine feet, six inches high, was carved from a single block of Italian marble. In her left hand she holds a rudder, symbol of navigation, and with the right hand she raises a crown of laurel.

At her feet, on the right side, is the eagle of the United States; on the left is a bomb, in memory of the bombardment. The height of the monument, including the statue, is fifty-two feet, two inches, and it is constructed entirely of marble. The entire monument is enclosed by an iron railing with bronze cannons at each corner.

The inscriptions on the base of the column read:

[North Side]
Bombardment
Of Fort
McHenry
13th September, A.D. 1814
And the Independence
Of the United States
The Thirty-Ninth

[South Side]
Battle of North Point
12 September A.D. 1814
And the Independence
Of the United States
The Thirty-Ninth

The names of the three officers inscribed:

James Lowry Donaldson, Adjutant 27th Regiment; Gregorius Andree, Lieutenant, 1st Rifle Battalion: and Levi Clagett, 3rd Lieutenant, Nicholson's Artillerists

The names of the thirty-nine enlisted men inscribed:

J. Clemm, T.V. Beeston, J. Haubert, J. Jephson, J. Wallace,
J.H. Marriot of John, E. Marriot, Wm. Ways,
J. Armstrong, J. Richardson, B. Bond, C. Cox, C. Bell,
T. Garrett, H.G. McComas, W. McClellan, J.C. Byrd,
D. Wells, J. K. Cox, B. Neal, B. Reynolds, D. Howard, U. Prosser,
A. Randall, R.K. Cooksey, J. Gregg, J. Evans, G. Jenkins,
W. Alexander, G. Fallier, J. Burneston, J. Dunn, P. Byard,
J. Craig, J. Merriken, I. Woolf, and D. Davis

CONGRESSIONAL MEDAL OF HONOR MEMORIAL

Location: Howard and Dolphin Streets
Designer: Memorial Craftsmen of America
Erected: 1939

Congressional Medal of Honor recipients Charles Hazeltine Hammann and Henry Gilbert Costin are honored by this memorial for their heroic actions while serving their country in World War I.

In July 1939, the Memorial Craftsmen of America, a trade organization specializing in tombstone construction, offered to erect a memorial in the city to an outstanding citizen of Baltimore. The selection criteria included three qualifications. The person must have been outstanding in a particular field or endeavor, did not already have a tombstone or memorial and was deceased. The organization selected Ensign Hammann and Private Costin after they were nominated by members of the American Legion and Veterans of Foreign Wars.[255] City officials were enthusiastic about receiving the memorial, and the municipal art commission recommended the plot of land at the intersection of Howard and Preston Streets as a location.[256]

About one thousand persons attended the dedication of the memorial on August 17, 1939, including members of the Hammann and Costin families. A parade from Battle Monument Square to the site preceded the ceremony. The program opened with a brief invocation by Reverend Father Ignatius Feechley,

Congressional Medal of Honor Memorial, Howard and Dolphin Streets. *Photo by author.*

189

Maryland State Chaplain of the American Legion. Alex Parker, secretary of the Memorial Craftsmen of America, presided over the ceremony. Paul Stevenson, president of the Memorial Craftsmen of America, presented the memorial to Maryland governor Herbert O'Connor. A closing benediction was given by Reverend Raymond W. Cook, a former department chaplain of the American Legion. The ceremony concluded with the playing of taps.[257]

When plans were developed for the Mount Royal Plaza renewal project in 1964, it became necessary to relocate the memorial. As such, it was moved to Howard and Dolphin Streets, about 375 feet north of its original location. The Maryland National Guard rededicated it on September 12, 1964, with Mayor Theodore McKeldin giving a short address.

The plain granite column is nine feet high and four feet wide. Insignias of the American Legion, Veterans of Foreign Wars, the Twenty-Ninth Infantry Division and the army and navy surround the upper part. A simulated flame surmounts the top.

The inscription on the memorial reads:

> CHARLES HAZELTINE HAMMANN
> ENS. AIR SERVICE U.S. NAVY
> MARCH 16, 1892–JUNE 14, 1919
>
> HENRY GILBERT COSTIN
> PVT. CO. H. 115TH INF. 29TH DIV.
> JUNE 15, 1898–OCTOBER 8, 1918
>
> ENSIGN HAMMANN RESCUED A FELLOW
> PILOT BY LANDING HIS SEAPLANE ON A
> SMALL BODY OF WATER NEAR POLA, AUSTRIA
> AUGUST 21, 1918
>
> PRIVATE COSTIN WAS KILLED IN ACTION
> DURING THE MEUSE ARGONNE OFFENSIVE
> WHILE SILENCING AN ENEMY MACHINE GUN
> NEST OCTOBER 8, 1918
>
> THE CONGRESSIONAL MEDAL OF HONOR
> WAS AWARDED THESE HEROES, NATIVES OF
> MARYLAND FOR EXTRAORDINARY PERFORMANCE
> BEYOND THE CALL OF DUTY, AND THEIR
> HEROISM IS HEREBY RECOGNIZED

JOHN EAGER HOWARD MONUMENT

Location: Washington Place, North Charles and Madison Streets
Designer: Emmanuel Fremiet
Erected: 1904

When this monument to Revolutionary War hero and fifth governor of Maryland John Eager Howard (1752–1827) was erected in 1904, it became the first equestrian statue erected in the city of Baltimore. The monument stands on part of the land that Howard donated to the city for the Washington Monument. Howard achieved fame at the Battle of Cowpens on January 11, 1781, by leading his soldiers in a brilliant bayonet attack and overwhelmed a superior British force. The attack changed the tide of the battle and saved the American Army.

In 1880, when the Maryland legislature declined to place a statue of Howard in Statuary Hall of the U.S. Capitol, a movement was started to erect a monument to the famous Marylander. Seeking to correct what it perceived to be an injustice, the board of directors of the Municipal Art Society of Baltimore passed a resolution to "erect a statue of John Eager Howard in some suitable place in Baltimore."[258] Following up the resolution to secure the necessary funds, the society formed the Howard Statue Committee consisting of W.W. Spence, Charles Fisher, William Keyser and William Marburg. The society itself contributed the initial $1,000 and raised the remaining funds through popular subscription.

In November 1901, a committee consisting of society members W.W. Spence, Theodore Marburg, L. Leroy White and Josias Pennington commissioned French sculptor Emmanuel Fremiet to design and create an equestrian statue at a cost of 60,000 francs. As a location, the committee selected the north end of the square in Washington Place, at the intersection of North Charles and Madison Streets.[259] The design, as well as the location, received the approval of both the municipal art commission and the park board.[260]

Dedication of the John Eager Howard Monument occurred on January 16, 1904, attended by a large crowd, including Maryland governor Edwin Warfield and Mayor Robert McLane. The ceremony preceding the unveiling was held in the main auditorium of the Peabody Institute due to inclement weather. A band opened the exercises by playing a medley of patriotic songs, including "The Star-Spangled Banner." Theodore Marburg presided over the ceremony and introduced the main speakers, Dr. Daniel C. Gilman of the Johns Hopkins University and Julian L. White of the Municipal Art

John Eager Howard Monument, Washington Place, North Charles and Madison Streets. *Photo by author.*

Society of Baltimore. Following the addresses, the crowd moved outside and proceeded to the monument site. Upon arrival, James R. Morris Howard, a representative of the Howard family, lowered the American flag that covered the statue.[261]

The bronze statue depicts Howard in the uniform of a Continental army officer, mounted on a horse. His right arm is outstretched with index finger pointing, as if leading soldiers in battle. The statue is twelve feet in height and surmounts a granite pedestal thirteen feet in height.

A bronze reproduction of a medal given to Howard by Congress in commemoration of the valor he displayed during the Battle of Cowpens is located on the back of the pedestal. On the obverse side of the medal is displayed a representation of a cavalry officer in the Continental army with uplifted saber riding down on the flag bearer of the enemy, who are in retreat. The Goddess of Victory is flying by the horseman's side, holding a wreath of laurel over his head. The Latin inscription on the face of the medal reads "John Eager Howard, *Legionis Praefecto, Comitia, Americina,*" which translated means "To John Eager Howard, Colonel of Infantry, the American Congress."

On the reverse side of the medal is a laurel wreath encircling the Latin inscription "*Quod in Nutantem Hostium Aciem Subito Irrens Praeclarum Bellcae Virtuis Specimen Dedit in Pugna*, Cowpens, XVII January, MDCCLXXXIL." Translated, it means "For his having given a noble example of martial virtue in the Battle of Cowpens, on the 17th of January 1781, when he heroically charged the wavering line of the enemy."

The inscription on the pedestal reads:

JOHN EAGER HOWARD
1752–1827

JOHN EAGER HOWARD MONUMENT

Location: Howard and Centre Streets
Designer: David L. Gerlach
Erected: 1985

This bronze sculpture grouping was erected in honor of Revolutionary War hero John Eager Howard (1752–1827). It serves as the centerpiece of Howard's Park, a triangular half acre of land located on Centre Street, between Howard and Eutaw Streets. Maryland artist David L. Gerlach created the work after being commissioned by the Municipal Art Society of Baltimore and the Market Center Development Corporation. The park itself is situated on a small parcel of land that was once part of the 250-acre estate that belonged to John Eager Howard.

Dedication of the park and monument occurred on July 29, 1985, presided over by Mayor William Donald Schaefer. The ceremony included performances by the U.S. Army Old Guard, the Commander-in Chief's Guard, a colonial color team, a fife and drum corps and the U.S. Army Band.[262]

The sculpture depicts a battle scene in which Howard, with sword drawn, is giving orders to three soldiers with rifles aimed in firing position. The figures, each about seven feet in height, surmount a base two feet, six inches in height.

The sculpture has a silicone bronze coating that gives the work a special golden color so appropriate to the subject, as General Nathanael Greene of Revolutionary War fame once wrote of Howard, "He deserves a statue of gold."

John Eager Howard Monument, Howard and Centre Streets. *Photo by author.*

The inscription on the bronze tablet reads:

THIS PARK AND SCULPTURE COMMEMORATE REVOLUTIONARY WAR
HERO, BENEFACTOR AND STATESMAN JOHN EAGER HOWARD. HOWARD
ENTERED THE REVOLUTIONARY WAR AT AGE 24, AND SOON GAINED
MILITARY FAME FOR HIS SKILLFUL AND HEROIC USE OF THE BAYONET
IN THE BATTLE OF COWPENS. AFTER THE WAR, HE SERVED
AS MARYLAND SURVEYOR, JUDGE, SENATOR, AND GOVERNOR.
THIS PARK REPRESENTS BUT A SMALL PIECE OF THE FOREST
THAT ONCE BELONGED TO HOWARD. HIS MAGNIFICENT 250 ACRE
ESTATE COVERED MOST OF DOWNTOWN BALTIMORE, STRETCHING
IRREGULARLY FROM NEAR ST. PAUL STREET NORTH TO BIDDLE
STREET, AND FROM THE JONES FALLS AT READ STREET WEST TO
EUTAW STREET. THE ESTATE PROPERLY CALLED "HOWARD'S PARK," WAS
USED FOR GENERATIONS AS A SCENE OF PROMENADES, PICNICS,
MILITARY EXERCISES, AND EVEN A DUELING GROUND. THE
DISMANTLING OF THE ESTATE WAS IN LARGE PART DUE TO THE
GENEROSITY OF HOWARD HIMSELF, WHO GAVE LAND FREELY FOR THE

CAUSES IN WHICH HE BELIEVED. HIS GIFTS FOR CIVIC CAUSES
INCLUDE THE LAND FOR THE WASHINGTON MONUMENT, LEXINGTON
MARKET, SEVERAL FIREHOUSES, AND EVEN A CEMETERY FOR
STRANGERS. TO RELIGIOUS GROUPS, HE WAS ECUMENICAL AS HE WAS
GENEROUS, GIVING LAND FOR THE CATHEDRAL AND SEVERAL
CHURCHES. HOWARD STREET WAS NAMED FOR HIM. EUTAW STREET
WAS NAMED FOR ONE OF HIS BATTLES.
THE SCULPTURE OF HOWARD LEADING HIS INFANTRY INTERPRETS
A TRIBUTE PAID TO HOWARD BY NATHANIEL GREENE OF
REVOLUTIONARY WAR FAME WHO WROTE OF HIM, "HE DESERVES A
STATUE OF GOLD, NO LESS THAN THE ROMAN AND GRECIAN HEROES."
HOWARD DIED ON OCTOBER 12, 1827 AT 75 YEARS OF AGE

Mayor William Donald Schaefer
and the Citizens of Baltimore
David L. Gerlach, Sculptor
Market Center Development Corporation
Richard N. Stern, Chairman
Robert Tennanbaum, President, Architect
The Delta Group, Landscape Architects
Municipal Art Society of Baltimore
Glen Gery Brick

CASIMIR PULASKI MONUMENT

Location: Patterson Park, Eastern and Linwood Avenues
Designers: Hans Schuler, A.C. Radziszewski
Erected: 1951

Revolutionary War hero Casimir Pulaski (1748–1779), often referred to as "Father of the United States Cavalry," is honored by this monument, which stands in Baltimore's Patterson Park. Pulaski is widely recognized for bringing order to American cavalry, using modern training methods that were still being used by the U.S. Army well into the twentieth century.

Casimir Pulaski arrived in America from Poland in July 1777 and joined the Continental army. Shortly thereafter, he was made chief of cavalry with the rank of brigadier general by Congress. Most of the men under his command were recruited in Baltimore. Casimir Pulaski died on October 11,

1779, after being mortally wounded during the Battle of Savannah. By act of Congress, October 11 is observed as Pulaski Day.

The idea of a monument honoring Casimir Pulaski was first proposed in 1929, when Mayor William Broening appointed a committee for the purpose and named former mayor James Preston as chairperson.[263] Patterson Park was selected as the location, and ground was broken on October 11, 1929, the 150th anniversary of Pulaski's death. François Pulaski, a grandson of the Revolutionary War hero, turned the first spade full of dirt.[264]

Baltimore sculptor Hans Schuler was commissioned to design and create the monument, and Baltimore architect A.C. Radziszewski was chosen to design the setting.[265] The expected cost was $60,000, of which the State of Maryland pledged $15,000 and the City of Baltimore pledged $15,000. The remaining $30,000 was raised by the Pulaski Monument Committee and the Polish community of Baltimore. The goal was achieved through public subscription, luncheons, receptions and other events.[266] Schuler and Radziszewski completed the design in February 1930, and it was approved by the municipal art commission.[267]

A scale model was put on display throughout several business sections of the city and was well received by the public. Construction of the monument was about to begin when several events occurred that caused setbacks to the project. Shortly after the foundation was laid in 1932, the Park Bank, which held the funds for the monument, failed. Undaunted, the Pulaski Monument Committee tried again to raise the necessary funds. In November 1939, the goal was achieved.[268]

Another delay occurred with the entry of the United States into World War II, when the government commandeered all bronze for military purposes. By the time the war ended in 1945, the original estimate of costs had increased. This made it necessary to use government funds to complete the project. Both the city and state governments generously contributed $10,000 to supplement contributions made by Baltimore's Polish community.[269] Work was completed in 1950, and both the municipal art commission and the park board gave their approval.[270]

Dedication of the Casimir Pulaski Monument occurred on October 14, 1951, exactly twenty-two years after its conception. The ceremonies were preceded by a parade led by Colonel William Baxter, commander of the One Hundred Seventy-Fifth Infantry Regiment. Other participants included the American Legion, various Polish organizations, school drum and bugle corps and the Two Hundred Twenty-Fourth Field Artillery. George S. Robertson, secretary of the Pulaski Monument Committee, opened the

Casimir Pulaski Monument, Patterson Park, Eastern and Linwood Avenues. *Photo by author.*

exercises. Reverend Bonaventure Santor of St. Stanislaus Catholic Church gave the invocation.

Members of the Lutnia Polish Chorus, wearing colorful native costumes, sang "The Star-Spangled Banner" and the Polish national anthem. Frederck Stieff, chairperson of the Polish Monument Committee, formally presented the monument to Mayor Thomas D'Alesandro Jr. In his address, the mayor stated, "All Americans hope and pray that the Polish nation who gave us Pulaski…may soon realize complete freedom."

Following the mayor's address, floral wreaths were laid on the monument by many organizations. Governor Theodore McKeldin delivered a short address and described Pulaski as a man who hated "the ways of the tyrant beyond the distant horizon as well as at his own doorstep."

Other speakers included Charles Ridgely, president of the Maryland Society, Sons of the American Revolution; Mrs. George Musgrave, state regent of the Society of Daughters of the American Revolution; General Reckford of the Maryland National Guard; and Frank Markiewicz, honorary president of the Polish American Citizens Committee. Several thousand spectators gathered around the stand and watched as Jean Goralski of the Polish Women's Alliance and George J. Robertson III of the Children of the American Revolution unveiled the monument.[271]

The Casimir Pulaski Monument consists of a bronze bas-relief, set in a thirty-foot square of marble. It depicts General Pulaski leading a cavalry charge.

The inscriptions on the monument read:

[Front]
1748—BRIGADIER GENERAL COUNT CASIMER PULASKI—1779
HERO OF THE AMERICAN REVOLUTIONARY WAR FATHER OF
AMERICAN CAVALRY

[Back]
Hans Schuler   A.C. Radziszewski
Sculptor   Architect

Thomas D. Alesandro, Jr.
Mayor, City of Baltimore

RODGERS BASTION MONUMENT

Location: Patterson Park, Patterson Park Avenue and Pratt Street
Designer: Unknown
Erected: 1914

The Rodgers Bastion Monument commemorates a series of military earthworks that fortified Hampstead Hill (now Patterson Park) used in the defense of Baltimore during the War of 1812. It was dedicated in 1914 as part of the centennial celebration of the writing of "The Star-Spangled Banner."

In September 1814, fresh from pillaging Washington, D.C., an armada of British warships intended to make Baltimore its next target. Baltimore, however, was ready. The city established a line of earthworks northeast of the city, along the crest of Hampstead Hill and down to the harbor. Overall, the line had sixty-two guns supported by more than ten thousand troops. Several hundred navy gunners were stationed at a crucial section of the line named Rodgers Bastion after their commanding officer, Commodore John Rodgers. Fortunately, the American defenders at Fort McHenry and North Point repelled the British attack, and Rodgers Bastion did not see any action.

Rodgers Bastion Monument, Patterson Park Avenue and Pratt Street. *Photo by author.*

The monument consists of seven cannons. Five of them are lined together side by side and face southeast toward the harbor, as they did in September 1814. Each of the five cannons is mounted onto a concrete base about three feet, six inches in height. Chiseled into the middle of each base is the date 1814. There is a sixth cannon located just behind these. It protrudes from the ground and faces the sky, with a cannonball lodged into its barrel. Located just a few yards to the west is a seventh and final cannon. It is a naval cannon of 1812 vintage and one of the original guns used in Rodgers Bastion. This cannon stood for many years projecting from a cement walk on Patterson Avenue at Boyer Street. How and when it arrived there remains a mystery. In August 1914, the National Star-Spangled Banner Centennial Commission received approval from the mayor and municipal art commission to place the cannon in Patterson Park.[272] This cannon also faces southeast and has a dedicatory bronze tablet attached to it. Beneath the cannon, there is a rectangular stone base measuring approximately eighteen inches in height, thirty-six inches in length and thirty inches in width.

Dedication of the Rodgers Bastion Monument took place on September 12, 1914, exactly one hundred years after the Battle of Baltimore. More than three thousand people attended the ceremony, including Mayor James Preston. The unveiling was performed by the mayor's son, Wilbur Preston.

Reverend Dr. Dewitt Benham delivered an address, as did Clymer P. White, a great-nephew of Commodore Rodgers. Mayor Preston accepted the monument on behalf of the city.[273]

The inscription on the bronze tablet reads:

THIS CANNON MARKS
RODGERS BASTION
WHICH FORMED PART OF A CHAIN OF
FORTIFICATIONS EXTENDING FROM THE
RIVER FRONT TO AND BEYOND THE SITE OF
THE PRESENT JOHNS HOPKINS HOSPITAL
MANNED IN PART BY AN AUXILIARY NAVAL
FORCE UNDER THE IMMEDIATE COMMAND OF
COMMODORE JOHN RODGERS.
THESE, WITH OTHER TROOPS, AMOUNTING
TO SOME 12,000 MEN WITH 100 GUNS
WERE UNDER GENERAL SAMUEL SMITH,
COMMANDER-IN-CHIEF OF ALL FORCES IN THE FIELD

ERECTED BY THE
NATIONAL STAR-SPANGLED BANNER CENTENNIAL COMMISSION
1914

SAMUEL SMITH MONUMENT

Location: Federal Hill Park
Designers: Hans Schuler and W. Gordon Beecher
Erected: 1918

Overlooking Baltimore's Inner Harbor stands a bronze statue of Samuel Smith (1752–1839), a major figure in Baltimore and Maryland during the early days of the Republic and a person who exercised significant influence in national affairs. In addition to being a decorated soldier, distinguished legislator, secretary of the navy and contributor to Baltimore's commercial prosperity, Samuel Smith served as the city's eleventh mayor. He won the gratitude of the citizens of Baltimore as the commander who successfully defended the city against the British during the War of 1812.

In 1915, the National Star-Spangled Banner Centennial Commission had surplus money remaining in its account. At the suggestion of Mayor James Preston, the commission decided to erect a monument in honor of Samuel Smith with the unused funds.[274] The commission selected Baltimore artists Hans Schuler and W. Gordon Beecher to design and create it at a cost of $5,000. The statue is the work of Schuler, and the architectural setting was done by Beecher.

On Independence Day 1918, the monument in honor of Samuel Smith was formally dedicated at its original location in Wyman Park, North Charles and 29th Streets. The ceremony was attended by Mayor James Preston, city officials and thousands of citizens. Arthur Bibbins, chairperson of the National Star-Spangled Banner Centennial Commission, presided over the event, which was preceded by a parade. Two large American flags covered it, with the Baltimore and Maryland State flags on each side. Several floral wreaths were situated at the base.

The exercises opened with everyone singing "America," followed by an invocation from Reverend Dr. Henry Branch, chaplain of the Maryland Society, Sons of the American Revolution and Society of the War of

Samuel Smith Monument, Federal Hill Park. *Photo by author.*

1812. Judge Henry Stockbridge, former president general of the National Society, Sons of the American Revolution, delivered the main address. He called Smith "Maryland's most distinguished citizen and soldier." Mayor Preston also made a short address and presented the monument to George Washington Williams, who accepted it for the park board. Samuel Yeardley Smith, a direct descendant of Samuel Smith, unveiled the statue.[275]

The monument stood in Wyman Park until 1953, when it was moved to Samuel Smith Park at the Inner Harbor. Three years earlier, Mayor Thomas D'Alesandro Jr. announced that it seemed fitting that the monument be "moved to the general's own park."[276] Several civic organizations opposed the move, and it touched off a small controversy.

Paula Schuler, wife of the sculptor, wrote a letter to the mayor stating that "moving the monument to an entirely inadequate location is a crime against Mr. Schuler's artistic expression."[277] At the time, the Inner Harbor was an area of dilapidated wharfs and warehouses. In 1953, the park board gave its approval to the move over all objections.[278]

In 1972, the monument was relocated to Federal Hill Park. It was to remain there until the completion of a waterfront promenade, where it would be placed permanently. This, however, was never done, and it can be seen today on top of Federal Hill.

The bronze statue stands nine feet, six inches in height and depicts Smith dressed in the uniform of an American general at the time of the War of 1812. It rests on a granite base.

The inscriptions on the base read:

[Front]
MAJOR GENERAL
SAMUEL SMITH
1752–1839

[Right Side]
UNDER HIS COMMAND THE ATTACK OF THE BRITISH
UPON BALTIMORE BY LAND AND SEA ON SEPTEMBER
12–14, 1814 WAS REPULSED
MEMBER OF CONGRESS
FORTY SUCCESSIVE YEARS
PRESIDENT U.S. SENATE
SECRETARY OF THE NAVY
MAYOR OF BALTIMORE

[Left Side]
HERO OF BOTH WARS FOR
AMERICAN INDEPENDENCE
LONG ISLAND
WHITE PLAINS
BRANDYWINE
DEFENDER OF FORT MIFFLIN
VALLEY FORGE
MONMOUTH
BALTIMORE

[Back]
Erected by the National Star-Spangled Banner
Centennnial Commission
James H. Preston, Mayor
President
Arthur B. Bibbons, Chairman
Robert E. Lee, Secretary
Jerome H. Joyce
John M. Deponai
Fredk. H. Gottlieb
Managing Directors
1917

Hans Schuler, Sculptor   H.P. Preger
W. Gordon Beecher, Arch. Builder

DANIEL WELLS–HENRY MCCOMAS MONUMENT

Location: Monument, and Aisquith Streets
Designer: Mills and Hanna
Erected: 1873

The city of Baltimore paid tribute to two local war heroes, Daniel Wells and Henry McComas, by erecting this monument in 1873. Both men are credited with having killed the British commanding officer Major General Robert Ross during the Battle of Baltimore in September 1814. Their action changed the course of the battle in favor of the Americans.

Daniel Wells–Henry McComas Monument, Monument and Aisquith Streets. *Photo by author.*

Daniel Wells, nineteen, and Henry McComas, eighteen, were riflemen in Captain Aisquith's company of sharpshooters when the British army landed at North Point, just east of Baltimore on September 12, 1814. During the skirmish with the front-line British, Wells and McComas saw General Ross approaching on his horse to observe the fighting. The two promptly shot and killed the general. When the British forces realized that their leader was dead, they raked the young men's position with a volley of musketry that killed the pair instantly. The demoralized British retreated and did not pursue the attack on Baltimore. The sharpshooters became heroes, and plans were made to honor their memory.

In March 1850, the First Baltimore Sharpshooters informed the mayor and city council that it had purchased a parcel of land at the intersection of Gay, Monument and Aisquith Streets, known as Ashland Square, for the purpose of erecting a monument to Wells and McComas.[279] A cornerstone was laid later that year. In 1851, the First Baltimore Sharpshooters donated the land to the City of Baltimore.[280] Three years later, in 1854, a fundraising campaign was started for the construction by the Wells-McComas Monument Association.

On September 9, 1858, the remains of Daniel Wells and Henry McComas were disinterred from their graves in Greenmount Cemetery and transferred to the hall of the Maryland Institute on Baltimore Street. There they laid in state under the care of an honor guard composed of Wells-McComas Riflemen. The catafalque occupied the center of the room where the bodies remained for two days and were visited by thousands of people.

On the morning of September 12, 1858, military units and civilian authorities formed a procession on Baltimore Street. Among those in the procession were Maryland governor Thomas Hicks, Mayor Thomas Swann and members of the city council. The coffins were removed from the Maryland Institute and placed on a funeral car. The procession moved along the streets of the city, with the bands playing a dirge, and ended at Ashland Square. An estimated twenty-five thousand people were in the square, and invited guests occupied a stage at the northeast corner of the square.

The exercises opened with a prayer by Reverend John McCron. Mayor Swann delivered an address, followed by the main speaker, Judge John C. Legrand. Upon the conclusion of Legrand's speech, the coffins were placed into an open vault in the ground, over which the monument was to be erected. While this was being done, a military unit fired three volleys over the remains, and the band played a solemn dirge, concluding the ceremony.[281]

The project stalled for twelve years without much progress being made. Then, in 1871, the base was erected with funds subscribed by various citizens.

In 1872, the city council passed a resolution providing $2,700 to complete the monument. The resolution instructed John C. Colley, the inspector of public buildings, to take charge of completing the project.[282] Colley, in turn, contracted with marble workers Mills and Hanna to complete the monument at a cost of $2,360.[283] The work was finally completed in May 1873.

The Wells-McComas Monument was dedicated on September 12, 1873, preceded by a military parade. The main speaker was General R.H. Carr, who praised the bravery and patriotism of Wells and McComas. The ceremony ended with General Carr reviewing the troops marching up Harford Road.[284]

The monument consists of marble obtained from quarries in Baltimore County. Its height from the ground is thirty-five feet. The base, comprising two granite steps, is laid on a brick foundation, underground, built over the remains of Wells and McComas. The pedestal is plain and square, ten feet high, having panels on the four sides. Upon this rises the obelisk, a tall, four-sided pillar tapering as it rises and cut off at the top in the form of a pyramid. The shaft is two huge stones, with a protecting cap interleaved, the lower one weighing fourteen tons and being four feet square at its base. The upper stone is eleven feet, six inches high, weighing eight tons. The obelisk is almost twenty-one feet in height; on the protecting stone between its two parts is carved in raised letters the names "WELLS AND McCOMAS."

The inscription on the monument reads:

[East Side]
DANIEL WELLS
BORN DEC. 30TH 1794
KILLED SEPT. 12TH 1814
AT THE BATTLE OF NORTH
POINT, AGED 19 YEARS
8 MONTHS AND 13 DAYS

[West Side]
HENRY G. McCOMAS
BORN SEPT. 20TH 1795
KILLED SEPT. 12TH 1814
AT THE BATTLE OF NORTH
POINT, AGED 18 YEARS
11 MONTHS AND 22 DAYS

NOTES

Chapter 1

1. BRG.51. S.5, Meeting Minutes, Baltimore City Board of Park Commissioners, October 4, 1944, Baltimore City Archives (hereafter cited as BCA).
2. BRG.36 S.1, Meeting Minutes, Baltimore City Board of Estimates, December 14, 1960, BCA.
3. Ibid., October 18, 1978, BCA.
4. *Baltimore Sun*, April 25, 1984.
5. BRG.36 S.1, Meeting Minutes, Baltimore City Board of Estimates, April 25, 1984, BCA.
6. *Baltimore Sun*, April 19, 1985.
7. *Baltimore Sun*, August 10, 1915.
8. *Baltimore Sun*, August 30, 1915.
9. BRG.9 S.15, Mayor James Preston Administration Files, document 95, 1915, BCA.
10. *Baltimore Sun*, June 16, 1916.
11. Meeting Minutes, Board of Directors of the Municipal Art Society of Baltimore, April 30, 1940, Archives of American Art, Smithsonian Institution, Washington, D.C., microfilm reel BA-1.
12. Ibid., October 28, 1941.
13. *Baltimore Sun*, February 4, 1942.
14. *Baltimore News American*, May 22, 1896.

15. *Baltimore Sun*, July 9, 1907.
16. *Baltimore Evening Sun*, April 26, 1921.
17. *Baltimore Evening Sun*, April 27, 1921.
18. *Baltimore Evening Sun*, October 19, 1921.
19. *Baltimore Evening Sun*, October 20, 1921.
20. *Baltimore News American*, May 30, 1930.
21. BRG.29 S.7, Meeting Minutes, Municipal Art Commission of Baltimore City, February 19, 1982, BCA.
22. A Committee of the Faculty, *Through the Years at Eastern High School* (N.p.: H.G. Roebuck and Son: 1944), 122–23.
23. BRG.16 S.1, Baltimore City Council Administrative Files, document 601 (1901), BCA.
24. *Baltimore Sun*, October 7, 1901.

Chapter 2

25. *Baltimore Sun*, April 28, 2012.
26. *Baltimore Sun*, June 30, 2012.
27. *Baltimore Sun*, July 15, 2012.
28. *Baltimore Sun*, August 11, 2012.
29. *Baltimore Sun*, September 7, 2012.
30. *Baltimore Sun*, September 29, 2012.
31. *Baltimore Sun*, October 23, 2011.
32. *Baltimore Sun*, September 4, 2014.
33. *Baltimore Sun*, May 16, 1995.
34. *Baltimore Sun*, October 21, 2002.

Chapter 3

35. The Board of Directors of the Maryland State Dental Association passed a resolution in favor of a monument honoring Chapin Harris on January 10, 1911. The seven-member fundraising committee was appointed on November 7, 1911. Minutes of the Board of Directors, Maryland State Dental Association, University of Maryland at Baltimore.
36. *Baltimore Sun*, March 2, 1922.
37. Ibid.
38. *Baltimore Sun*, March 9, 1922.

39. Ibid.

40. *Baltimore Sun*, June 2, 1922.

41. BRG.51 S.5, Meeting Minutes, Baltimore City Board of Park Commissioners, September 27, 1939, BCA.

42. BRG.16 S.5, Baltimore City Council Ordinance 266, May 8, 1907. See also: RG.16 S.2, Proceedings, Baltimore City Council, Second Branch, May 8, 1907, BCA. The Maryland legislature authorized the appropriation on February 21, 1908. See *Laws of Maryland*, Acts of Assembly, 1908, Chapter 24.

43. *Baltimore Sun*, May 8, 1908.

44. BRG.35 S.1, Contracts and Bonds, document 24, contract between the John Mifflin Hood Memorial Commission and Richard E. Brooks, June 24, 1908, BCA.

45. BRG.16 S.5, Baltimore City Council Ordinance 599, December 12, 1910, BCA.

46. *Baltimore Sun*, May 12, 1911.

47. Meeting Minutes, Board of Directors, Municipal Art Society of Baltimore, October 11, 1904, Archives of American Art, Smithsonian Institution, Washington, D.C.

48. Ibid., March 10, 1913.

49. Ibid., December 18, 1928.

50. *Baltimore Sun*, May 10, 1934. See also *Baltimore Sun*, May 13, 1934.

51. *Baltimore Sun*, September 19, 1935.

52. Meeting Minutes, Board of Directors, Municipal Art Society of Baltimore, May 24, 1900, Archives of American Art, Smithsonian Institution, Washington, D.C., microfilm reel number BA-1, frame number 40.

53. *Baltimore Sun*, January 10, 1906.

54. *Baltimore Sun*, March 3, 1906.

55. BRG.51 S.5, Meeting Minutes, Baltimore City Board of Park Commissioners, July 5, 1905, BCA.

56. *Baltimore Sun*, January 10, 1906.

Chapter 4

57. BRG.8 S.2, Baltimore City Commission for Historical and Architectural Preservation, Confederate Monuments Report, BCA.

58. Ibid.

59. WMAR2News, June 10, 2022, Baltimore, Maryland.

60. BRG.51 S.5, Meeting Minutes, Baltimore City Board of Park Commissioners, March 16, 1983, BCA.
61. *Baltimore News American*, February 19, 1984.
62. *Baltimore Sun*, October 19, 1984.
63. BRG.16 S.5, Baltimore City Council Resolution Number 130, 1899, BCA.
64. BRG.51 S.5, Meeting Minutes, Baltimore City Board of Park Commissioners, April 12, 1900, BCA.
65. Mrs. James MacClure Gillet, "I Remember....A Great Day for the Rebels," *Baltimore Sun*, February 15, 1953.
66. *Baltimore Sun*, May 3, 1903.
67. Resolution passed at the annual meeting of the Maryland Chapter, United Daughters of the Confederacy, December 7, 1911. See *Baltimore Sun*, December 8, 1911.
68. *Laws of Maryland*, Acts of Assembly, 1914, Chapter 476.
69. BRG.51 S.5, Meeting Minutes, Baltimore City Board of Park Commissioners, October 9, 1914, BCA.
70. *Baltimore Sun*, November 3, 1918.
71. Meeting Minutes, Board of Directors, Municipal Art Society of Baltimore, April 25, 1932, Archives of American Art, Smithsonian Institution, Washington, D.C., microfilm reel number BA-1, page 578.
72. Ibid., July 1, 1936, Archives of American Art, Smithsonian Institution, microfilm reel number BA-1.
73. Ibid.
74. *Baltimore Sun*, May 2, 1948.
75. BRG.9 S.23, Mayor Thomas D'Alesandro Jr. Administrative Files, document 108, 1948, BCA.
76. BRG.29 S.7, Baltimore City Department of Legislative Reference, Board of Recreation and Parks, February 28, 1979, BCA.
77. *Baltimore Fishbowl*, April 6, 2021.
78. BRG.9 S.3, Mayor's miscellaneous incoming correspondence, letter from William T. Walters to Mayor Ferdinand Latrobe, November 14, 1887, BCA.

Chapter 5

79. BRG.36 S.1, Meeting Minutes, Baltimore City Board of Estimates, March 31, 1914, BCA.

80. BRG.35 S.1, Contracts and Bonds, Contract File Number 2938, contract between David M. Andrew Company and the City of Baltimore, September 29, 1914, BCA.

81. *Baltimore Sun*, February 28, 1915.

82. BRG.69 S.3, Meeting Minutes, Board of Trustees, Community College of Baltimore, September 27, 1977, BCA.

83. Letter from Stanley Sollins, executive director of the Baltimore Jewish Council, to Mayor William Donald Schaefer, August 21, 1978, Mayoral records of William Donald Schaefer, BCA. See also *Baltimore Sun*, August 19, 1978.

84. BRG.62 S.3, Meeting Minutes, Baltimore City Architectural Review Board, Charles Center–Inner Harbor Development Corporation, Project Files, Holocaust Memorial, October 13, 1978, Box 189, BCA.

85. *Baltimore Jewish Times*, April 27, 1979.

86. *Baltimore Sun*, November 3, 1980.

87. *Baltimore Sun*, September 11, 1995.

88. Ibid.

89. *Baltimore Sun*, November 20, 2000.

90. *Capital Gazette*, September 11, 2011.

91. BRG.36 S.1, Meeting Minutes, Baltimore City Board of Estimates, October 1, 1975, BCA.

92. *Baltimore Sun*, May 15, 1988.

93. BRG.9 S.15, documents 49-B and 49-E(1), Mayor James Preston Administrative Files, Meeting Minutes, National Star-Spangled Banner Centennial Commission, May 5, 1914, BCA.

94. *Baltimore American*, September 12, 1914.

Chapter 6

95. BRG.9 S.13, Mayor E. Clay Timanus Administrative Files, document 115, 1906, BCA. See also *Baltimore Sun*, October 10, 1906.

96. BRG.16 S.2, Baltimore City Council Journal of Proceedings, October 15, 1906, BCA.

97. BRG.16 S.1, Baltimore City Council Administrative Files, document 670, Report of the municipal art commission, October 16, 1906, BCA.

98. BRG.35 S.1, Meeting Minutes, Baltimore City Board of Estimates, October 26, 1906, BCA.

99. BRG.16 S.1, Baltimore City Council Administrative Files, Report of the municipal art commission, January 14, 1907, BCA.

100. *Baltimore Sun*, June 10, 1907.

101. BRG.9 S.14, Mayor J. Barry Mahool Administrative Files, document 23, letter from State's Attorney Albert Owens to Mayor Mahool, June 8, 1907, BCA.

102. BRG.16 S.2, Baltimore City Council Journal of Proceedings, First Branch, May 4, 1908, BCA.

103. *Baltimore Sun*, November 22, 1908.

104. *Baltimore Sun*, December 11, 1985.

105. *Baltimore Sun*, March 26, 1987.

106. BRG.16 S.5, Baltimore City Council Ordinance 222, 1913, BCA.

107. BRG.35 S.1, Contracts and Bonds, document 29 (1913), BCA. See also RG.9 S.15, document 21C, Mayor James Preston Administrative Files, 1913, BCA.

108. *Baltimore Sun*, June 2, 1914.

109. BRG.36 S.1, Meeting Minutes, Baltimore City Board of Estimates, September 21, 1977, BCA.

110. *Baltimore Sun*, May 17, 1980. See also *Washington Post*, May 17, 1980.

111. BRG.48 S.76, Baltimore City Department of Housing and Urban Development, Art Project Files, 1977, BCA.

112. *Washington Post*, November 3, 2009.

Chapter 7

113. BRG.9 S.24, Mayor J. Harold Grady Administrative Files, document 24, correspondence between Mayor Grady and Cesar A. Rojas, Consul General of Venezuela, August 16, 1960, BCA.

114. BRG.51 S.5, Meeting Minutes, Baltimore City Board of Park Commissioners, October 25, 1960, and January 17, 1961, BCA.

115. BRG.9 S.24, Mayor J. Harold Grady Administrative Files, document 24, correspondence between Guilford Association President Gerald S. Wise and the Baltimore City Board of Park Commissioners, November 25, 1960, and correspondence between park board executive secretary Joseph J. King and City Solicitor Harrison L. Winter, November 29, 1960, BCA. See also RG.51 S.5, Meeting Minutes, Baltimore City Board of Park Commissioners, November 22, 1960, BCA.

116. *Baltimore Sun*, April 20, 1961.

117. *Claypole's Daily Advertiser*, August 22, 1792.

118. Christopher Columbus and the Discovery of America: An Address Delivered by Professor Herbert B. Adams of the Johns Hopkins University at the Peabody Institute, October 10, 1892.

119. BRG.51 S.5, Meeting Minutes, Baltimore City Board of Park Commissioners, September 10, 1963, BCA.

120. BRG.9 S.25, Mayor Theodore R. McKeldin Administrative Files, document 104, program of the Columbus Monument rededication, October 12, 1964, BCA.

121. *Baltimore Sun*, August 19, 1892.

122. *Baltimore Sun*, September 8, 1892.

123. BRG.51 S.5, Meeting Minutes, Baltimore City Board of Park Commissioners, September 7, 1892, BCA.

124. *Baltimore Sun*, October 13, 1892.

125. BRG.9 S.13, Mayor E. Clay Timanus Administrative Files, document 595, correspondence between Mayor Timanus and Theodore Marburg, December 1906, BCA.

126. BRG.16 S.1, Baltimore City Council Administrative Files, document 670, Report of the municipal art commission to the Second Branch, Baltimore City Council, January 14, 1907, BCA. See also BRG.16, S.2, Proceedings, Second Branch, Baltimore City Council, January 14, 1907, BCA.

127. BRG.16 S.5, Baltimore City Council Ordinance 95, April 24, 1908, BCA.

128. *Baltimore Sun*, April 25, 1907.

129. BRG.16 S.1, Baltimore City Council Administrative Files, document 465, report of the municipal art commission to the Baltimore City Council, March 2, 1908, BCA

130. *Baltimore Sun*, May 16, 1911.

131. *Acts of Congress, Statutes at Large*, Sixty-Third Congress, Session 1, Chapter 215 (1914).

132. Ibid.

133. BRG.9 S.15, Mayor James Preston Administrative Files, document 49-A2, Letter from the Francis Scott Key Monument Advisory Committee to Mayor Preston, March 12, 1915, BCA.

134. *Baltimore Sun*, September 22, 1916.

135. *Commercial and Financial World*, September 30, 1916.

136. BRG.9 S.15, Mayor James Preston Administrative Files, document 73-A3, U.S. War Department letter to Mayor Preston, March 23, 1918, BCA.

137. Ibid., letter from Secretary of War Newton D. Baker to Mayor Preston, August 3, 1918, BCA. See also *Baltimore Sun*, August 8, 1918.

138. *Baltimore Sun*, July 23, 1920.

139. *Baltimore Sun*, June 15, 1922.

140. BRG.9 S.15, Mayor James Preston Administrative Files, document 118-2, Resolution adopted by the Lafayette Monument Committee, 1917, BCA.

141. BRG.29 S.1, Baltimore City Department of Legislative Reference, Subject Files, Lafayette Statue, BCA.

142. BRG.9 S.16, Mayor William F. Broening Administrative Files, document B10-13, correspondence between Mayor Broening and United States Senator Orvington Weller, April 13–16, 1921, BCA.

143. *Baltimore Sun*, August 4, 1923.

144. BRG.26 S.1, *Baltimore Municipal Journal*, September 10, 1924, BCA. See also *Baltimore Evening News*, September 6, 1924.

145. BRG.9 S.15, Mayor James Preston Administrative Files, document 95-1, 1916, BCA. See also BRG.51 S.5, Meeting Minutes, Baltimore City Board of Park Commissioners, June 6, 1916, BCA.

146. *Baltimore Sun*, October 7, 1916.

147. BRG.9 S.14, Mayor J. Barry Mahool Administrative Files, document 327, BCA.

148. *Baltimore Sun*, December 1, 1893.

149. BRG.51 S.5, Meeting Minutes, Baltimore City Board of Park Commissioners, March 3, 1892, BCA.

150. Ibid., October 13, 1892, BCA.

151. *Laws of Maryland*, Chapter 113, January 6, 1810.

152. See J. Jefferson Miller II, *The Washington Monument in Baltimore* (Baltimore, MD: Peale Museum, 1966).

153. Ibid.

154. *Laws of Maryland*, Acts of Assembly, Chapter 102, 1815.

155. Ibid., Chapter 77, 1815.

156. See J. Thomas Scharf, *The Chronicles of Baltimore; Being a Complete History of "Baltimore Town" and Baltimore City from the Earliest Period to the Present Time* (Baltimore, MD: Turnbull Brothers, 1874), 375.

157. Letter from Henrico Causici to the Washington Monument Board of Managers, May 1827, Maryland Historical Society, MS 876, Box 1.

158. *Baltimore American and Commercial Daily Advertiser*, November 26, 1829.

159. Ibid.

Chapter 8

160. BRG.51 S.5, Meeting Minutes, Baltimore City Board of Park Commissioners, June 11, 1868, BCA.

161. Ibid., July 8, 1969, BCA.

162. BRG.9 S.26, Mayor Thomas D'Alesandro III Administrative Files, document 7, letter from Mayor D'Alesandro, ex-officio chairperson of the municipal art commission to James E. Lewis, October 29, 1968, BCA.

163. BRG.51 S.9, Meeting Minutes, Baltimore City Board of Park Commissioners, October 13, 1971, BCA.

164. BRG8 S.2, Meeting Minutes, Baltimore City Commission for Historical and Architectural Preservation, October 15, 1971, BCA.

165. *Baltimore Sun*, June 13, 1972.

166. BRG.51 S.5, Meeting Minutes, Baltimore City Board of Park Commissioners, December 20, 1932, BCA.

167. *Baltimore Sun*, April 24, 1933.

168. BRG.29 S.7, Meeting Minutes, Municipal Art Commission of Baltimore City, September 16, 1983, BCA.

169. *Baltimore Sun*, June 11, 1984.

170. Maryland General Assembly, Joint Resolution Number 3, Acts of 1985.

171. BRG.51 S.5, Meeting Minutes, Baltimore City Board of Park Commissioners, October 14, 1987, BCA.

172. *Baltimore Sun*, May 28, 1990.

173. Ibid.

174. Maryland Revolutionary War Patriots Monument letter, Maryland Society, Sons of the American Revolutionary war, November 15, 1892, Vertical File, Enoch Pratt Free Library, Baltimore, Maryland.

175. BRG.16 S.5, Baltimore City Council Ordinance 65, 1892, BCA.

176. Maryland House of Delegates Journal of Proceedings, page 1,003 (1892), and Maryland State Senate Journal of Proceedings, pages 99–100 (1892), Maryland State Archives.

177. BRG.16 S.1, Baltimore City Council Administrative Files, document 601, 1901, BCA.

178. *Baltimore Sun*, October 20, 1901.

179. BRG.9 S.14, Mayor E. Clay Timanus Administrative Files, document 384, 1906, BCA.

180. *Baltimore Sun*, April 22, 1925.

181. Budget of the State of Maryland, 1942: Miscellaneous Appropriation Number 2, General Fund, Governor's Allowance, Maryland State Archives.

182. *Baltimore Sun*, March 2, 1942.

183. *Baltimore Sun*, June 11, 1943.

184. BRG.73 S.1, Meeting Minutes, Baltimore City War Memorial Commission, removal of the Spanish mortar from the War Memorial Building to the site of the Spanish-American War Veterans Memorial, April 29, 1946, BCA.

185. *Laws of Maryland*, Acts of Assembly, Chapter 539, April 5, 1906.

186. *Baltimore American*, November 7, 1909.

187. BRG.16 S.5, Baltimore City Ordinance 185, December 6, 1906, BCA.

188. BRG.51 S.5, Meeting Minutes, Baltimore City Board of Park Commissioners, September 4, 1906, BCA.

189. BRG.9 S.14, Mayor J. Barry Mahool Administrative Files, document 166, 1907, BCA.

190. *Baltimore Sun*, November 7, 1909. See also *Baltimore American*, November 7, 1909.

191. Maryland House of Delegates Joint Resolution 31, 1983 session, Maryland General Assembly, Chapter 22 of the Acts of 1984, Maryland State Archives.

192. *Baltimore Sun*, November 12, 1986.

193. *Baltimore Sun*, March 8, 1986.

194. *Baltimore Sun*, June 4, 1986.

195. *Baltimore Evening Sun*, November 12, 1986.

196. *Baltimore Sun*, May 29, 1989.

197. *Laws of Maryland*, Acts of Assembly (1894), Chapter 655, Section 37, page 1,053.

198. *Laws of Maryland*, Acts of Assembly (1896), Chapter 381, page 685.

199. BRG.16 S.5, Baltimore City Council Ordinance 30, 1902, BCA.

200. *Baltimore Sun*, April 29, 1902.

201. *Baltimore Sun*, July 30, 1903.

202. BRG.51 S.5, Meeting Minutes, Baltimore City Board of Park Commissioners, July 29, 1903, BCA.

203. *Baltimore Sun*, July 30, 1903.

204. BRG.13 S.1, Baltimore City Law Department, City Solicitor's Opinion Files, File Number 144, August 14, 1903, BCA.

205. *Baltimore Sun*, September 22, 1903.

206. *Baltimore Sun*, August 7, 1936.

Chapter 9

207. BRG.20, Meeting Minutes, Baltimore City Firefighters Monument Ad Hoc Committee, January 14, 1985, BCA.
208. *Baltimore Sun*, April 20, 1990.
209. *Baltimore Sun*, June 24, 1978.
210. BRG.26 S.3, *Baltimore Journal*, June 8, 1979, BCA.

Chapter 10

211. *Baltimore Magazine* (November 1963). See also *Baltimore Sun*, October 10, 1963.
212. *Baltimore News American*, March 13, 1973, interview with Betti Richard, creator of the Cardinal Gibbons statue.
213. *Baltimore Sun*, December 14, 1964.
214. *Baltimore Sun*, December 18, 1967.
215. *Baltimore Sun*, January 19, 1935, and June 20, 1935.
216. *Baltimore Sun*, November 1, 1936.
217. *Baltimore Sun*, October 24, 2008.

Chapter 11

218. BRG.31 S.1A, Meeting Minutes, Baltimore City Board of School Commissioners, October 5, 1944, BCA.
219. *Baltimore News Post*, "Bronze Captures Douglass' Spirit," November 13, 1956.
220. *Baltimore Afro-American*, October 20, 1956.
221. *Baltimore Sun*, April 8, 1890.
222. BRG.16 S.5, Baltimore City Council Resolution 183, June 2, 1884, BCA.
223. *Baltimore Sun*, April 28, 1885.
224. Ibid.
225. *Baltimore American and Commercial Advertiser*, September 23, 1885.
226. BRG.16 S.1, Baltimore City Council Administrative Files, document 375, letter to the mayor and city council from the Thomas Wildey Monument Committee, 1864, BCA.
227. BRG.51 S.5, Meeting Minutes, Baltimore City Board of Park Commissioners, November 1864, BCA.

228. BRG.16 S.1, Baltimore City Council Administrative Files, document 703, January 13, 1865, BCA.
229. *Baltimore Sun*, April 27, 1865.
230. *Baltimore News American and Commercial Daily Advertiser*, September 21, 1865. See also *Baltimore Sun*, September 21, 1865.

Chapter 12

231. BRG.16 S.1, Baltimore City Council Administrative Files, Mayor Jacob Small to the First and Second Branches of the city council, February 12, 1827, BCA.
232. BRG.16 S.5, Baltimore City Council resolution, March 24, 1827, BCA. See also BRG.16, S.1, Baltimore City Council Administrative Files, document 533, 1827, BCA.
233. BRG.16 S.2, Baltimore City Council Proceedings, Second Branch, January 7, 1828, BCA. See also BRG.16 S.5, Resolution Number 5, February 4, 1828, BCA, and BRG.16 S.1, Baltimore Council Administrative Files, document 613, February 4, 1828, BCA.
234. BRG.16 S.2, Baltimore City Council Proceedings, First Branch, February 3, 1879, BCA.
235. Ibid.
236. Ibid., February 25, 1879, BCA.
237. BRG.16 S.1, Baltimore City Council Administrative Files, opinion from Baltimore City Solicitor Thomas Hall to Mayor Ferdinand Latrobe, February 18, 1879, BCA.
238. BRG.16 S.2, Proceedings, Baltimore City Council, Second Branch, March 1, 1879, BCA.
239. *Laws of Maryland*, Acts of Assembly, Chapter 420, 1880.
240. BRG.16 S.2, Proceedings, Baltimore City Council, First Branch, January 31, 1881, BCA.
241. Ibid., September 27, 1881, BCA. See also BRG.16 S.1, Baltimore City Council Administrative Files, document 511, Mayor Ferdinand Latrobe to the city council, 1881, BCA.
242. BRG.16 S.5, Baltimore City Council resolution 136, May 3, 1882, BCA.
243. *Baltimore American and Commercial Advertiser*, September 13, 1882.
244. BRG.16 S.5, Baltimore City Council resolution 137, May 20, 1886, BCA. See also BRG.16 S.1, Baltimore City Council Administrative Files, document 1053), 1886, BCA.

245. *Baltimore News American*, September 13, 1914.

246. BRG.9 S.15, Mayor James Preston Administrative Files, Expenditures, National Star-Spangled Banner Centennial Celebration, 1914, BCA.

247. *Laws of Maryland*, Acts of Assembly, 1815, Chapter 102.

248. MS.3, Baltimore Monumental Subscription Book, 1815, BCA.

249. See J. Thomas Scharf, *History of Baltimore City and County* (Philadelphia, PA: Louis H. Everts, 1881), 267.

250. MS.1198, Battle Monument Papers, Letter from the principal co-signee, Barrell and Company, to James A. Buchanon and Elias Hore of the Battle Monument Committee, December 13, 1815, BCA.

251. BRG.16 S.1, Baltimore City Council Administrative Files, Articles of Agreement between John C. Neale, Frederick Baughman, Elias Hore and the Battle Monument Committee, December 13, 1815, BCA.

252. *Baltimore American and Commercial Daily Advertiser*, September 13, 1822.

253. BRG.16 S.1, Baltimore City Council Administrative Files, document 105, Report of the Battle Monument Committee to the mayor and city council, December 6, 1825, BCA.

254. BRG.16 S.5, Baltimore City Council Ordinance 12, February 2, 1827, BCA.

255. *Baltimore Sun*, July 21, 1939.

256. *Baltimore Sun*, August 9, 1939.

257. *Baltimore Sun*, August 18, 1939.

258. Meeting Minutes, Board of Directors, Municipal Art Society of Baltimore, April 27, 1890, Archives of American Art, Smithsonian Institution, Washington, D.C.

259. Ibid., November 27, 1901.

260. Ibid., January 7, 1902.

261. *Baltimore Sun*, January 17, 1904.

262. *Baltimore Sun*, July 30, 1985.

263. *Baltimore Evening Sun*, October 4, 1929.

264. *Baltimore Evening Sun*, October 12, 1929.

265. *Baltimore Evening Sun*, December 16, 1929.

266. *Baltimore Evening Sun*, February 19, 1930.

267. BRG.26 S.1, *Baltimore Municipal Journal*, February 21, 1930, BCA.

268. *Baltimore Sun*, November 15, 1939.

269. *Baltimore Sun*, October 16, 1950.

270. BRG.9 S.23, Mayor Thomas D'Alesandro Jr. Administrative Files, document 219, 1950, BCA.

271. *Baltimore Sun*, October 15, 1951.

272. BRG.9 S.15, Mayor James Preston Administrative Files, document 49E-5, National Star-Spangled Banner Centennial Commission, 1914, BCA.

273. *Baltimore American*, September 13, 1914.

274. BRG.9 S.15, Mayor James Preston Administrative Files, document 95(3), 1915, BCA.

275. *Baltimore American*, July 5, 1918.

276. *Baltimore Evening Sun*, September 1, 1950.

277. BRG.9 S.23, Mayor Thomas D'Alesandro Jr. Administrative Files, document 12, 1950, BCA.

278. BRG.51 S.5, Baltimore City Board of Park Commissioners, May 29, 1953, BCA.

279. BRG.16 S.1, Baltimore City Council Administrative Files, document 518, 1850, BCA.

280. BRG.16 S.5, Baltimore City Council Ordinance 49, 1851, BCA.

281. *Baltimore American and Commercial Daily Advertiser*, September 14, 1858.

282. BRG.16 S.5, Baltimore City Council Resolution 348, 1872, BCA.

283. BRG.3 S.1, Baltimore City Commissioners Administrative Files, 1873, BCA.

284. *Baltimore American and Commercial Daily Advertiser*, September 13, 1873.

BIBLIOGRAPHY

Primary Sources, Archives and Libraries

Acts of Congress, Statutes at Large.
Archives of American Art, Smithsonian Institution.
Baltimore City Archives.
Enoch Pratt Free Library.
Laws of Maryland, Acts of Assembly.
Maryland State Archives.

Newspapers

Baltimore Afro-American.
Baltimore American and Commercial Daily Advertiser.
Baltimore Jewish Times.
Baltimore Municipal Journal.
Baltimore New American.
Baltimore News Post.
Baltimore Sun.
Capital Gazette.
Claypole's Daily Advertiser.
Commercial and Financial World.
Washington Post.

Reports

Report of the Special Commission to review Baltimore's Public Confederate Monuments, Baltimore Commission for Historical and Architectural Preservation.

Secondary Sources

Adams, Herbert. *Christopher Columbus and the Discovery of America.* An address delivered by Professor Adams of the Johns Hopkins University at the Peabody Institute, October 10, 1892.

Miller, J. Jefferson, II. *The Washington Monument in Baltimore.* Baltimore, MD: Peale Museum, 1966.

Scharf, J. Thomas. *The Chronicles of Baltimore, Being a Complete History of "Baltimore Town" and Baltimore City from the Earliest Period to the Present Time.* Baltimore, MD: Turnbull Brothers, 1874.

———. *History of Baltimore City and County.* Philadelphia: Louis H. Everts, 1881.

ABOUT THE AUTHOR

*T*homas Cotter is a retired archivist with the National Archives and Records Administration (NARA), where he served twenty-five years as an appraisal archivist. Prior to joining NARA, he served as an archivist with the Baltimore City Archives for seven years. A native Baltimorean, he is a graduate of the University of Baltimore with a bachelor's degree in U.S. history and a master's degree in legal studies. He currently lives with his wife, Sharon, in Hagerstown, Maryland. In his free time, he enjoys hiking the Appalachian Trail near his home. He also enjoys spending time with his family, including his wife, two daughters and their husbands and two granddaughters.

Visit us at
www.historypress.com